TREK!

Man Alone in the Arizona Wild

The Desert Journals of Geoffrey Platts

With an introduction by
Marshall Trimble
Arizona Author & Historian.

Man Alone in the Arizona Wild

First edition

Platts, Geoffrey.
TREK! / by Geoffrey Platts.
p. cm.
ISBN 0-9631487-0-2
1. Nature. I. Title.

Manufactured in the United States of America
9 8 7 6 5 4 3 2
First Edition

The author will tithe a portion of the proceeds from the sales of his book to the Earth.

Remembrance

In fond memory of my late friend
Edward Abbey (1927-1989), author and true American,
who did his damnedest for the desert — and inspired us all.
His last words: "I did what I could."
Indeed he did.

Contents

The Dance

(for Geoffrey P.)

The sunlight slants late in December
as if in reaching under
she warms the sleeping desert
hidden safely under stone.

The eve of the solstice
at dusk the dance begins anew

And I wonder if your cabin
is in shadow yet,
the canyon calling it a day earlier.

But I know you are dancing
a desert dance without equal
and a voice remembering
always what it never forgot.

A low song sung
listening to the rocks
as the creek washes and rolls
each sound

and it returns in joy,
for your desert song and dance
form the path to her heart.

You bear her scars boldly
and she your song proudly.

In Hell's Canyon
the dance never ends
and our songs together
planted in rock crevices with sweat
have already sprouted.

We shall return to see her flowers.

— Jeffrey Cooper, desert *compañero*
December 22nd 1987

Dedicatory

For Madrecita

...and for Sioux, who knows how deeply I love her.

Acknowledgments

Earnest thanks to Jack Grenard, new friend and publisher, for his faith in these journals and his respect for my philosophical idiosyncracies.

To Ralph Sullivan, *amicus fidelis*, for his calm counsel along the way.

To Tom Blaney, photographer and devout caretaker of the Earth, for his striking cover picture.

To Carl Muecke, my friend of thirty years, who captures with his pen (page 44) the humor of a very serious business.

And lastly, appreciations to Hans Gilsdorf, artist-friend of the Earth, for his Sonoran sketch (page *x*) inspired by our wildlands hike.

Foreword

.....Well pleased to recognize
In Nature and the language of the sense,
The anchor of my purest thoughts, the nurse,
The guide, the guardian of my heart,
And soul of all my moral being.

— William Wordsworth, "Tintern Abbey"

These journals are, quite simply, my love letters to the Sonoran desert. All were written while on summer solo treks which, with the passage of a dozen years, have become a sort of annual pilgrimage to me. A Walking in Beauty, as the Navajo people say. A gazing outward at that Beauty surrounding me — and a looking inward also. And, perhaps most importantly, just a "being in the here and now."

May these writings help spark some fresh awareness of the elemental need to wholly protect the one and only Sonoran desert. For its own sake and then for ours.

Autumn 1991

Publisher's Note

> Camerado, this is no book.
> Who touches this touches a man.
>
> — Walt Whitman

The chapter titles in Spanish — and other sprinklings of *español* in the journals — are an honoring of that lyrical language Geoffrey Platts has come to know and to love. Likewise, the British spelling usage — *colour* for *color*, for example — the reader finds in the earlier journals reflects an old habit the author found hard to break. For sentimental reasons, these remain "uncorrected."

Publication of these journals coincides with the thirtieth anniversary of the start of journal writing by the author when, in 1961, he set off around the world with a hometown friend and chronicled the adventure.

The author warmly invites letters to Post Office Box 2568, Carefree, Arizona 85377.

Introduction

I first met Geoffrey Platts back in the late 1970s when he wanted to discuss ways we might jointly resist newly-arrived developers who were systematically casting uncontrolled destruction on the Sonoran desert. His premise was to create a greater awareness of the natural beauty, and at the same time educate newcomers and natives alike on the delicate nature of the desert. We were an unlikely pair — I was dressed in cowboy boots, hat, and faded jeans, looking more like a redneck refugee from the Sagebrush Rebellion than a historian. Geoffrey was wearing khaki trousers and shirt, resembling one of Montgomery's North African soldiers. I was a native Arizonan. He had arrived from England in 1962. I regaled large groups with songs, stories, and cowboy poetry. He was a thoughtful seeker of solitude and silence. A mesmerizing speaker, he had a wonderful way of painting word pictures, his British accent dramatizing the metaphorical imagery. I was also quite impressed by his sincerity and arranged for him to present a dramatic reading of one of his solitary sojourns into the desert before a group of students at Scottsdale Community College.

Several months later, on a hot summer afternoon, I drove by yet another new development carved out of the desert. This one included man-made lakes ("a little piece of Minnesota right here in Arizona") with homes complete with Disney Desert landscaping. Standing near the entrance was the solitary figure of Geoffrey Platts, carrying a sign protesting more destruction of the desert. I was so inspired, I got out of my pickup and joined him. Before long, several others had joined us. We lost that battle, and a few others over the next few years, including legislative bills on bottle return and native trees, but the thought of relinquishing the desert without a fight never occurred.

During this time Geoffrey continued his lonely treks into the desert, recording his thoughtful reflections. "Go into the desert," he told me, "and sit quietly. Soon the noises of the city will be expunged from your body, your mind will go free, and your spirit will lift itself. The desert will come alive all around you." I did and found truth in his words. I had lived in the Sonoran desert all my life but had never come to acceptable terms until then. This formidable, seemingly indestructible land also had a fragile, sensitive side. Although it is unforgiving to those who taunt it, the desert demands very little from those who come to find solace on its terms.

In the years that followed, we continued to share from our cornucopia of resources. I introduced Geoffrey to Edward Abbey and a friendship developed that lasted until Abbey's death in 1989. Geoffrey introduced me to the Arizona Nature Conservancy and eventually I became a board member.

Geoffrey likes to remind me of how much I have done for him, but on the contrary, it was this Englishman who hailed from a land so far away and so vastly different, who awakened in me a greater awareness of my native surroundings — how precious this wonderful land is and how it must be preserved for future generations — and how I must use my influence to speak out.

If I have been any good, I owe that to him.

Marshall Trimble
Scottsdale, Arizona

The deserts should never be reclaimed. They are the breathing spaces of the West and should be preserved forever.

— John C. Van Dyke, *The Desert*, 1901

Something hidden.
Go and find it.
Go and look behind the Ranges.
Something lost behind the Ranges.
Lost and waiting for you.
Go.

— Rudyard Kipling

I: Hombre de la Cueva: Cave Dweller

Monday May 15th 1978

By 11:30 a.m., having concealed the Luvmobile behind a riparian thicket, I was at the trailhead. It was a hot yet hazy day with the temperature going for the hundred (100-degrees F.) mark. I considered the two roadrunners (chaparral cocks) spotted earlier a good omen for this five-night outdoors experience.

It was my intention to return to a cave previously shopped for and there to spend a working week as a latter-day troglodyte. I'd always had this urge, possibly primæval, to live in a cave for a while. My backpack felt uncommonly heavy — not surprising given the amount of food (see list, next page) I'd decided to carry. Therefore getting to the canyon was more work than pleasure but I made myself reflect positively on my good fortune at having the healthy legs, strong back, and long wind to be able to do such a hike. To be safe, I hand-carried a 1.5-gallon plastic jug of water which, at twelve pounds, began to get burdensome after not long; my other hand was occupied with the lugging of a plastic pail containing three cans of corned beef hash, two of chili beans, two of sardines, and one of pear halves. In short, I was overloaded. Yet rather that than go hungry, felt I. So I trudged and sweated, rested and drank.

Finally at 2 p.m., with aching shoulders and a throbbing brow, I arrived — and by the grace of God and *Madre Naturaleza* the creek was still running with "cool, clear water" (as the song goes). It was however noticeably down from the last time I was here — these hundred-degree temperatures take their toll on water sources. Before climbing the hillside to my cave, I rested a while, washed my face and limbs in the creek, and drank

Outside temp., 3 p.m., 87°

deeply. Then up and on with the dead-weight pack and upwards to where I judged the cave to be. (It wasn't visible from the lower stretch.) I misjudged and got tangled up in chaparral (scrub oak), which was both exhausting and aggravating. After disentangling and finding the correct cliff, I checked in to the cave, bag and baggage, at 2:20 p.m. What a relief to unburden, remove boots and relax.

Once rested, I then set about putting my cave in order. The floor had to be swept and cleared of the dried dung (cow, coyote, and probably "cat") which was old enough to be odourless.

Provisions & Equipment
carried for the five-day cave experience, Monday May 15th to Saturday May 20th 1978

3 15oz. cans corned beef hash
2 15oz. cans chili beans
2 3oz. cans sardines
1 15oz. can pear halves
2 pkgs. Japanese noodles
1 lb. granola
1 1.5-lb. loaf wheat bread
1 lb. brown sugar
1 cup brown rice
1 12oz. pkg. raisins
1 bag dried peaches
1 lb. processed cheese slices
2 pkgs. oatmeal cookies
6 bananas
3 onions
2 garlic & chewing gum
6 oranges
9 hard-boiled eggs
peanuts in shell
chiltepines
6 fresh tomatoes
6 fresh carrots
green onions
tea bags
dried milk
orange drink powder
2 plastic garbage sacks
tent (unnecessary)
sleeping bag
sleeping pad (foam)
small pillow
hunting knife
eating utensils
2 cooking pans
soap/toothpaste/T-brush/razor
space blanket
jeans (for evening)
plastic pail
1.5-gallon water-jug
half-gallon water-jug
mosquito netting
lightweight can-opener
gym shoes
monocular (for bird watching)
10 half-candles
empty sardine can
1 small circular fire grill
emergency medical supplies
snake-bite kit
3 paperback books
paper & pen
2 shoulder satchels
thermometer
mosquito coils

Made up a sleeping-bag space in the farthest corner and, at the other end, dug a small firepit. The roof of the cave bore carbon evidence of ancient fires; it is said that such blackening of rocks will remain for hundreds (if not thousands) of years.

No signs of human occupancy (Indian, pioneer, or recent) other than these fire marks. No potsherds, arrowheads, or even beer cans. Nevertheless, lizards — one without a tail and another with a striking black-and-orange collar — bees, flies, gnats, and mosquitoes are actively in residence here. Also a scorpion which I startled by removing the rock that was his cover and sanctuary; he fled into a cave-crevice. (He was not *Centruroides sculpturatus*, the sharpest stinger among desert scorpions.) The bees, which for some reason I've yet to ascertain, cling to the ceiling and buzz around now and again, have ignored my large presence, happily.

In size, the cave is approximately eighteen feet wide and no more than six feet deep: the cliff overhang above its mouth ensures that rain doesn't dampen the dryness of its interior. The "doorway" faces east in the tradition of Navajo hogans; thus the early morning sun will be a stand-in for an alarm clock. It's possible (at the end near the opening) to stand up straight, but toward the north end the ceiling slopes and one must bend. Where the sleeping bag lies, a failure to stoop brings a bang on the cranium. I stood three mesquite branches up against the overhang and am now furnished with excellent hanging racks — for satchel, towel, socks, toilet roll, boots, bandanna. A square of flat rocks near the fire pit provides a cook's stool and food tables, raised above ant level. (No ants as yet but they may invade at the whiff of scraps and tidbits.)

Upon completing initial cave-dwelling chores, I sat back, unravelled, and admired the new abode and its glorious view to the east. The gnats and midges were pestilential today but more so outside than inside. For the first time ever, I gave a serious tryout to Vicks VapoRub, applying it stickily to face, neck, ears, arms, and legs. I do believe that it discourages major attacks by flying insects. They still hover about the head and shoulders but keep their distance more. Also remembered to bring along oriental-style mosquito coils which smoulder for hours, giving off fumes supposed to be death-dealing to mosquitoes; I lit one at 4 p.m., put it back in a corner of the cave, and, thanks to its disagreeable effects on the airborne visitors, was able to write this journal without discomfort.

The sunset was not extravagant but, rather, serene. I stood at the mouth of *mi cueva* and let this sense of serenity wash gently over me like a wavelet. There were sounds, several of them — the wail of quail as they called to one another in the jojoba-chaparral, the piping of a male cardinal resplendent in his scarlet coat, the melancholy cooing of mourning-doves, the scolding chatter of a cactus wren perched atop a wickedly-spiked cholla, even the high- pitched whine of a mosquito freshly ventured forth on her evening blood patrol — but they too were subdued in accord with this evening's setting of the sun. Later came the sounds of low hooting of perhaps a great horned owl, the orchestrated chirruping of crickets, and the swish of bats' wings as their busy owners (first one spotted at 7:26 p.m.) set forth to satiate their voracious appetites for insects-in-flight. They're Mexican free-tailed bats, I believe. Supper at 6 was corned beef hash with chopped onions, rawgarlic, and chiltepines — very savoury and nobody within miles to consider me unsavoury of breath after eating it. Also boiled a quarter-panful of quick brown rice and washed the lot down with black tea. Oatmeal cookies supplied the dessert.

Temperatures:
65° — 6 a.m.
82° — 1 p.m.
76° — 6 p.m.

Bats are truly the only flying mammals on earth — besides man — and far from blind.

Wrote by two-candlepower light, which did attract several moths, oneofthemsuicidally—"likea mothtotheflame." I'verationed myself to two half-candles per evening. Tonight's quota burnt much too rapidly, perhaps because they were heat-softened during the afternoon hike.

Tuesday May 16th 1978

No callers during the moonlit night, though I did hear the snapping of twigs and rustling of bushes a time or two. First light came at 4:40 a.m. and I was up an hour later. The mosquitoes seemed more active in the early morning than during the warm night. They sang a lot but stung little. I did have a square of fine-mesh netting to drape over my head and upper torso.

Orange and a squeezed half-lemon and water for breakfast. Descended to the creek before the sun had penetrated the canyon and, a few minutes before 7 o'clock, was already trudging farther back into these mountains, with a maximum of five morning hours of hiking in mind. Followed the old road which, to my satisfaction, became more unnavigable and rutted as it twisted through the canyon. It was a bright and lovely day tempered with a steady breeze, and I enjoyed the uninterrupted solitude to the utmost. Both sides of the canyon were flanked with lofty buttes, pinnacles, and sawtooth rock formations ranging in time-worn colour from burnt-orange to greyish purple. Here and there, glancing upwards at these massive ridges, I would spot remote caves, their black mouths beckoning me to explore them. The shimmering sun reached down to touch me at 7:15 a.m., dispelling most of the shade in the lower reaches. It stayed deliciously cool before that time. The creek flowed sporadically, never dry for too long a stretch, and the trail regularly cut across it. Beside a sun-whitened coyote scat lay another so fresh that Brother Coyotl (Aztec [Nahuatl] spelling) must've been ahead of me by mere minutes. But though my eyes scrutinized the talus slopes to left and right, I could see neither hide nor hair of him.

Some embankments were densely covered with wild buckwheat, its pale cream flowerheads growing in rosette form; the seeds of this low bush-like plant were milled into flour by the earlier Indians, it is said. The brittle bush (*incienso*) which runs riot in over-grazed areas has by now gone to seed. As I brushed by it the still-intact pods would rattle in a most disconcerting way. In the middle of the meandering road there were often swaying tall thistles, those regal emblems of Scotland, whose pale lavender flowerheads, cherished by swallowtail butterflies, were actually eye-high as I passed. Lizards, alarmed by my footsteps, continually scampered to safety beneath some wayside bush. One nervous little creature was either bathing (do lizards like water?) or had fallen into the creek because, as he streaked away from me at dazzlingly high speed, he was gleaming wet. Though the spring wildflowers are still, at this late day in May, in evidence here and there, their moment of glory has passed and been handed over to the gorgeously golden palo verde (called by Mexicans *lluvia de oro*, golden rain), to the radiant-orange flowertips of the coachwhip ocotillo, and to the cacti. The giant saguaros' waxy-white bloom is beginning to show (much to the instinctual joy, no doubt, of the whitewing doves who feed off them and help pollinate), and three species of cholla — cane, buckhorn, and teddy bear — are now flowering, golden, blood-red, and pale-yellow, respectively. Nor must I forget to mention *opuntia*, the common prickly pear, whose exquisite bloom is large, rose-like, and of a deep yellow hue. One *opuntia* I noticed had enormous pads the size of those found in the heart of the Sierra Madre.

Well-shaded gullies seemed to be choked with jojoba (pronounced ho-HO-bah and once, five years ago, referred to as

JE-hovah by a friend!), the females of which are this year carrying nuts (still green and unripe) that are plump and plentiful. My cave entrance is ringed by these bountiful bushes.

After I'd hiked at a relaxed pace for an hour and a quarter, the road took an upward direction, bringing me to a long-forgotten cabin site; nothing remained but some broken pieces of sun-discoloured glass and badly rusted strips of metal. A pretty area, however, with tall shade trees: cottonwood, sycamore, and even Arizona walnut. Without a doubt — a perennial source of water — along the edges of which grew stands of seep-willow, the feathery French tamarisk (salt-cedar), hackberry, black willow, and the omnipresent mesquite trees. Because of a strong showing of sugar sumac (whose berry-coating the Indians used for a sweetener) crowding the steep slopes above the dwelling site, I guessed that the road had climbed close to 3,000 feet. Not a single juniper, though.

Walnut trees = nogales, in Spanish

Pressing on, with the intention of turning around and retracing footsteps at 9:30 a.m. (two and a half hours of hiking in each direction), I kept to the "farmtrack" and it wended out of the deeper, more spectacular canyon into hilly, rolling desert. The creek still trickled but no stately water-loving trees here. It was of interest to observe that the banana yucca (*baccata*) were making their annual and miraculous change from flower to fruit. The mass of pendulous creamy-white blossoms on a stem (pollinated at night by the pronuba moth in a highly-specialised symbiosis with the yucca, until recently considered a member of the lily family) gives rise to the popular name of Our Lord's Candle. Here too grew an occasional agave (century plant) sending up its caudex — or central stalk — after gathering sufficient energy and sugars over a period of some ten to thirty years. Once it has resolved to thrust forth its flower-stalk, it sets in motion not only its long-awaited moment of glory but its death process. Having blossomed and seeded, it dies. How enlightened society would become if its beings (all of us, that is) came to regard death as the noblest moment of life. But didn't the Romans (and Greeks?) devote their lives to the concept of dying "the good death?"

By 9:30 a.m. I found myself out of the canyon completely and atop a windswept hill overlooking a deep valley traversed by several maintained dirt roads, coming from and going to I know not where. No vehicles on them and no other traces of human habitation. But on this hilltop there were fences, a gate and some lowing cattle: rancher's range, doubtless. More tyre tracks along this open stretch and the wide circle of rocks ("whiteman's campfire") which had not been scattered after use. One such camp circle, along with the inevitable beer cans, milk carton, and other disgusting trash, had newspaper strewn about it; the date on this faded, torn newspaper (*Arizona Republic*) read October 17th, Sunday, 1976. Almost nineteen months ago to the day, these pigs had left their mess. By crushing the aluminum cans flat and lengthwise, I was able to carry out, by hand and in the satchel, nearly all that I came across during the morning. The amount wasn't excessive but still too much for an area of such singular natural beauty.

An old saying goes, "Whiteman build big fire, stand back, stay cold; Indian build small fire, sit close, stay warm."

On this treeless knoll, with its broad, uncluttered vista, the curious parasite dodder had taken a stranglehold on a number of small bushes. Dodder is a Medusa's head of orange-yellowish tendrils which envelop the host bush, sapping its life force and literally choking it. Dodder apparently starts on the ground with a flimsy root system and there, once firmly enfolded around an unfortunate bush, pulls up its roots and lives entirely aloft.

Wildlife sightings were few: a pair of timid cottontails, possibly a pyrrhuloxia (a grosbeak resembling a female cardinal), definitely a phainopepla (the mistletoe-loving, black-crested flycatcher who perches high to snatch at insects in the air; believe that I can now identify its single-note call), and certainly, most striking, a hooded oriole (yellow with black tailfeathers, face, and throat). Heard a warbling vireo gaily doing what his name suggests — but couldn't clap eyes on him — an elusive, plain, undistinguished bird but what splendid singing he does. Oddest creature was a creek spider who spun his or her web just above the water's surface, anchored it on dry rocks, and then clung to it upside down; not only that but he or she conducted all affairs — crawling, fleeing, weaving, and eating — in that topsy-turvy manner. Saw it devour an entrapped fly. What mandibles!

I was back at home base fifteen minutes before midday. As the sun reached its zenith, I bathed naked by the creek, soaping and rinsing myself well away from the pure water and afterwards sitting in the flowing stream. What refreshingness. What a childlike feeling of utter freedom, however momentary. After this desert baptism (made possible by an aquatic grant from that most bounteous of sponsors, Mother Earth), I lay lizard-like on a boulder, basking and sun-drying. Washed the sole pair of shorts, filled the gallon-and-a-half plastic jug with water and panted up the loose dirt, scrub-dotted slope to the cave. It was lunchtime by then and, having had no more than an orange since rising at 5:45 a.m., I ate heartily. Lunch finished, I propped myself up on the back wall of my cliff dwelling (in the central part or living room, one could say) and applied pen and memory to writing this account. But within minutes my eyelids began to droop and weariness overcame me. Uncharacteristically, I took a ninety-minute siesta and enjoyed giving in to the early-afternoon drowsiness. Resumed writing in the mid-afternoon and continued, with a break now and again, until dinnertime. During one interlude, I made a half-hearted attempt to scale the cliff above the cavemouth but gave up after chunks of rock came away in my hand. Possible to climb but perilous.

Bright and hot burns mesquite wood, so supper of chili and beans — with cheese slices and chopped onion and garlic — and sweet black tea was ready in no time. Dessert consisted of granola, dried milk, and fresh creekwater. *¡Sabroso!* Treated to a sunset display of aerial acrobatics by a team of twittering cliff swallows (who fly crazily like bats and also take their insect meal on the wing. In fact, a swallow's flight is simply one endless meal.) To the left of my elongated natural doorway, hopping inquisitively in and out of rock crevices, came a canyon wren, who saluted the swift-falling darkness with his distinctive and captivating call, a series of descending trills. Canyons and this active brown-and-white-breasted bird with bobbing tail go hand-in-hand in harmony.

9:30 p.m. — all's well and cool, 71° F — in the cave. I'm writing by the light of one candle which, in this sleeping area recess, is sufficient. From time to time, small innocuous bugs will stroll across the page and a moth will madly dive-bomb into the flame. The curling smoke from the green allethrin coil appears to be keeping all mosquitoes at bay. They were numerous all day long — peculiar, because they're supposed to be more nocturnal than diurnal in activity. This cave variety is not as blood-lusting as most, luckily; but they certainly can sing. The half-moon rides high and bright but its beams have yet to irradiate the cave's interior. The light from the flickering candle casts my shadow black and giant-like against the rear rock wall. There's a coziness to my cave, even a primitive sense of security; I am happy, grateful, and fortunate to be here now — in the here and now.

Wednesday May 17th 1978

Having read till 11 p.m. last night, I didn't rise up before 7 a.m. No nocturnal noises or intruders, but still I slept only fitfully. At 7:08 a.m. the morning sun struck the back wall of the cave, compelling me to move the two bags of food (wrapped in plastic garbage sacks, which diminish odour and discourage probing by skunks) to the yet-shaded inner recess. Aired the sleeping bag over a jojoba bush at the mouth of the cave, brushed teeth above the latrine pit which I'd dug with an empty oval sardine can (good makeshift digging tool and also serves as a sand-filled candle-holder), and washed the pans which I'd soaked overnight. A handful of dried cowdung was put to use as a pan-scourer — effectively, too. The one-and-a-half gallons of water brought up to the cave each noon suffice for a day's drinking, cooking, and toothbrushing, if used sparingly. A few paces away from the opening, I was intrigued to find the remnants of a rattlesnake which appeared to have been devoured by some other creature, for nothing of it was left except the tell-tale hollow rattle and pieces of dry vertebrae. Of live snakes I've seen nothing so far, but I'm nonetheless stepping cautiously and utilising a stick as bush-prodder, particularly when doing desert detours off the beaten path. When I was last here, three snakes made an appearance — a coontail rattler, a four- to five-foot racer with a black back and a pink underbelly, and a curled charcoal-coloured critter with dirty white bands (later identified as a desert kingsnake).

At 8 a.m. I set off downstream intending to do a full morning's hike. I soon picked up a rough road winding to the rear of the mountain which houses my cave. High above me, soaring and wheeling effortlessly was Old Zopilotl (turkey vulture), scanning the desert for carrion. Much as I like vultures, I'd no intention of personally obliging this one in its graceful quest. Within close air-distance, a red-tailed hawk — obviously at peace with his vulture neighbor — sailed majestically in the sky looking for live rather than dead prey. Passed a giant saguaro, one of whose arms had lately fallen off. On the arm's tip still freshly grew a delicate white flower, smaller in circumference than the flowers of some lesser cacti, strangely. These solitary sentinels of the desert seem to be unaffected by the loss of a limb or even part of the main trunk. The topmost section of one had buckled and developed a hole through which daylight gleamed — and yet its flowerbuds grew healthy and numerous. Sadly, several of these giants have toppled earthwards, having absorbed excessive water during the torrential February and March 1978 rains and become bloated.

On this trail I came upon a packrat's nest so well fortified as to be virtually impregnable. It had been built, painstakingly, in the middle of a patch of prickly pear cactus which was in turn entangled with cat-claw acacia. What a choice of homesites by that astute defender, the packrat, sometimes known as trader rat for its habit of stealing glittering objects and putting in their stead a shard of glass or an old nail. Yesterday I lifted up rock on a cairn (probably a mining claim) and flushed out a packrat — quite unintentionally. It scurried off into some brush, choosing one of several exits from its nest woven into the pile of rocks.

In less than an hour this wagon road came to an end; the turnaround point was, inevitably, a repository for beer cans. Close by grew an extraordinary saguaro whose arms had dropped to a twisted, swirling position around its "waist." I cut across-desert to reach the saddle a short distance away and was afforded a sweeping view of *bajada*, narrow valley, and, beyond, a sun-parched sierra of great dimension. Hadn't planned on retracing footsteps so soon in the morning but, with no confirmed

source of water ahead of me, it wasn't wise to begin bushwhacking. On the way back, the high-pitched whistles of young verdins in mesquite had me on the lookout with monocular to eye. Then a mockingbird, the first I've seen hereabouts, indulged in a session of impudent song-mimicry; related to curve-billed and other thrashers, mockingbirds are equally bold and brazen. I've even observed mockingbirds (in the city) swoop on cats that've approached too near to their nests.

A little way down the hill, just off the road, stood a stock tank (with a date inscribed in the concrete: 12-6-67) filled with water but slimy with algae; no cattle in the vicinity, but the water not entirely going to waste this morning, for a whitewing dove was drinking there. Though spring-fed, by way of a sunken pipe, the creek alongside the tank was as dry as a bone. I followed it a hundred yards up the arroyo just to make sure.

Arriving back at least an hour before noon, I decided to walk a mile upstream to a spot where the water ran over a quartz terrace into a pellucid pool. Took along a plastic bucket, washcloth, razor, and soap and had a standing bath followed by a sitting splash-and-soak in the pool itself, much in the Japanese communal bath fashion, actually. Delicious sensation. How cold that springwater was. A curious gila woodpecker, apparently outraged by this display of clotheslessness, let out a shrill croak and flew off to peck elsewhere. A stone's throw away from my *baño* was a salt-cedar (French tamarisk) in feathery, wispy, delicate, pale-mauve flower and, mid-creek, a luxuriant young cottonwood, most secure in its water supply. I shaved and, before going in to lunch, washed my only shirt and the bandanna, spreading them to dry on the smooth boulders — much as the washerwomen do in India, at the river's edge. Today the fleas were ferocious, myriads of them massing on my legs and arms. The repellent effect of Vicks VapoRub seemed to last for far too short a time.

As early as high noon, the sun had passed above the cave, leaving it in the coolness of shade. How ideally located. Lunch of a melted (processed) cheese and onion sandwich and a brace of boiled eggs was eaten, therefore, in comfort, and the afternoon spent in bringing this cave-record up to date.

Don't know if the thermometer is functioning properly or not, but in the last three days it hasn't recorded a temperature above 85° F. At six o'clock I started fire for supper, which became corned beef hash, diced onions, and garlic — plus two bruised and battered tomatoes which wouldn't have survived another day. Milk and granola for dessert — and of course a billycan full of black tea. Last summer in the Sierra Madres (Sonora, Mexico) friend Michael and I ate only bully beef, beef stew, potatoes, and rice for a full month; somehow we never sickened of those staples —maybe because we were leading a vigorous camping life. And because we had no other choice.

While wolfing down my food in true caveman fashion, I was excited to notice a lion within yards of me — not a mountain lion, mind you — merely that bizarre dust-kicking tiny insect called the ant-lion. It was creating a cunning ant trap, shaped in the dust like a perfect inverted cone; a death-pit, in fact, for should any wandering ant fall into it, there's little chance of escaping a rather horrible fate. As the ant slips downward into the pit, the lion, lurking hidden beneath it, commences to toss loose earth in every direction so that the wretched ant slithers and slides in a futile attempt to climb out. Eventually it wearies and falls prey to the jaws of the buried ant-lion, which makes an instant meal of it. (In Sonora, Mexico, in the summers of '76 and '77, our beach campsite was, each morning, pitted liberally by these ant-lions.)

9 p.m.: An insect-free night so far. Invariably the flies and those accursed gnats cease to function when darkness falls; presumably they rest up for the first-light assault. In desert

First bat, 7:26 p.m.

9 p.m. temperature, 69° F.

terrains these winged pests seem more active in the daytime than at night (even the local mosquitoes) whereas in the tropics the reverse applies. Time to read a book, *The Ebony Tower*, by John Fowles. The canyon glows bright with moonlight. Candle out at 10 p.m.

Thursday May 18th 1978

7 a.m., 68°

Daybreak around 4:40 a.m. Ten minutes later, the flies — as if orchestrated by a conductor — began buzzing busily. Strong gusts of wind bent the bushes in front of the cave but, inside and well-sheltered, I felt nothing more than a cool breeze stroke my face. Lit a mosquito coil but did not bestir myself till 7 a.m. Sun pierced the interior at 7:08 a.m.; I relocated the bundles of food and then, as a precaution, I left a note explaining the direction of my hike-to-be. In view of the well-concealed cave entrance and the fact that its specific location is known only to me, perhaps the writing of that note was completely meaningless. This morning, after easing down the slope to creek level, I determined to follow another track up a side canyon; although its course was still visible (though faintly) the desert had reclaimed the width of it with grasses, wildflowers, and other small plants. Because it had undergone no vehicle use for a number of years, there wasn't a scrap of garbage its entire length. Roads in use = people = garbage. It's as simple as that. Was this an old mining road, I wondered? Probably, for now and then I'd come across rock-cairns which appeared to be claim markers. On one ridge had been sturdily built a wall of yellow rock; no mortar had been used, just the old drywalling technique often seen on the Yorkshire moors. (Yorkshire stone, however, is not yellow and orange, merely a dull grey in keeping with the weather.) I didn't comprehend the purpose for the wall. Within one hundred yards was a lively spring supporting a grove of sizeable willow trees and a sole cottonwood. This area didn't lack for water, at least in mid-May. After a few miles of meandering, the road was finally swallowed up by a tangle of brush.

Choosing to scramble up a slope to gain broader vistas, I disturbed a coontail rattlesnake who spotted me (and I it) at a distance of two yards. Looking at me balefully, it decided on a discreet flight and slid under a jojoba bush without even rattling. A very pleasant way of behaving, which ensured that both of us lived to see another day of roaming in our cherished desert. Rattlesnakes, like people, have widely differing temperaments; the one I happened upon a week ago dashed under a bush, took up an aggressive coiling stance and didn't stop rattling for fifty minutes. In fact, I went ahead and ate dinner to his noisy tune. Today's *vibora de cascabel,* toward whom I felt nothing but good will, did make a peculiar whining noise as he moved off. Have never heard that before.

In little more than a half-hour, I came upon another western diamondback, this one curled up sound asleep on a shaded shelf of rock. A picture of perfect peacefulness. The yellows and browns of its markings were beautifully bright. It took not the slightest notice of me and dozed on. I was happy to meet with these two "lords of life" and can honestly say that, thanks to their benevolent non-involvement, neither of the encounters had me rattled. Wandering cavewards down the same track, I succumbed to the temptation of clambering up a steep (but not precipitous) buckwheat-strewn slope that began up high at the base of a cliff with intriguing rock formation. After thirty minutes of sweating effort, I found myself in a protected funnel scooped out of the main escarpment by the winds of ages and which, had it a roof or shelf above, would've been a cool and con-

"Lords of life," from the D. H. Lawrence poem, "Snake"

cealed cave. Rock-climbed from there to the backbone of the ridge and my eyes were greeted by a breath-catching panoramic view of range after range of redrock mountains reaching to infinity. And how forcefully the wind blew up on those time-honoured heights.

Chancing upon what I believed to be a white mariposa lily growing in solitary splendour near the summit was similar, I suppose, to the joy of finding an eidelweiss after an alpine climb. Here too grew barrel cacti, broad of girth and armed with red-tinged fishhook spines; one already bore a crown of yellow fruit, edible but nowhere as palatable as that of other cacti (prickly-pear, hedgehog, saguaro — and especially organ-pipe, *pitahaya*).

Descended by way of a more gradual but long incline carpeted with the dead-seeming resurrection fern, so parched that it brittle-crunched underfoot. Extraordinary little plant, for it goes lifelessly dormant during hot, dry spells but, upon absorbing a good rain, it revivifies itself and becomes brilliant green, springy, and mosslike. From the most hopeless appearance to the vividly verdant, in such a short space of time. Truly inspiring.

Packrats do use ingenuity, no doubt about it. This a.m. I glimpsed a nest that had been built in a narrow fissure half-way up a sandstone bank; somehow the resident rodent had dragged up there needle-pointed teddy bear cholla joints (that, under sunshine and in the distance, deceptively resembled soft fuzz-balls) and he'd arranged them as a barricade of spearpoints around the tight opening to the crevice. Nothing in God's creation could endanger that rat and its young when on the inside of their fierce fence.

Shortly after 11 a.m. I stood at the clearwater pool and, without much ado, slid in it. Previous customer, who left with undignified haste, was an iridescent green lizard, six inches long at least, with a black and red collar. (Saw three of these gaudies today.) My great hulk of a body (comparatively speaking) caused measurable agitation amongst the tadpoles occupying the pool; but soon they became inured to my wallowing and returned to their curious huddling and overcrowding in the shallows. Tried a cold-water hair shampoo, moderately successful. Am enjoying this post-hike midday bath appointment. This deepest of the small creek-pools is twenty-five minutes away from the cave.

This is the fourth day of being removed from civilization ("syphilisation," as Aldous Huxley called it), and I have slipped comfortably into a basic pattern of living: up with the sun (as it comes into my cave), down to the creek and off on a full morning's exploratory hike, bathing and laundering just before the noon hour, then hauling water up the hill, lunch at 12:30 p.m. or so, and the remainder of the afternoon and evening free for reading, writing, ruminating, and relaxing. Is a life pattern a prerequisite for all beings, no matter where or how they live? Perhaps the insistence on a structured, organized manner of living is essentially a whiteman's blessing (affliction?).

Picking out pebbles, I made smooth a square of dirt-floor and, resting my back against the uneven rear wall of the cave (furnished with handy if bumpy and slanting shelves on which balance my bits and pieces), sat and wrote throughout the afternoon. Once in a while I'd stretch my legs and gaze across the saguaro-rich canyon and up at the round and lonely juniper growing in isolation a thousand feet above me on the opposite skyline. An unmistakeable tree even at that elevated distance. On one occasion a pressing visit to the latrine trench took the local cliff-hanging grey lizard by surprise. Not until he'd recovered his composure did he begin to do his comical push-ups — not at all comical to him, though; he was in dead earnest displaying his territorial maleness to me. I was duly impressed and intimidated and beat a respectful retreat.

Supper sustaining but not too imaginative — chili beans with still-fresh onion and garlic, solidified by a bowl of granola, milk, raisins, and sliced banana. And tea.

A cloud-hazy evening sky added dimension to the colouring effect of the sinking sun; its last rays illumined the great redstone buttes on the far side of the canyon, and I watched in silent reverence and with profound gratefulness for what I had been given. Already high in the sky, the waxing moon lost no time in silvering the night after it had fallen.

By the light of one candle I wrote and read, stretched out in the sleeping nook, till 10 p.m.

Friday May 19th 1978

Rose up at 6:45 a.m. No animal rustlings or disturbances during the night. Could it be that the primitive precaution of my peeing on all the larger rocks ringing the cave entrance really worked? A coyote (or even domestic dog), for example, defines his territory in such a fashion, although he makes it more obvious still by depositing scat on top of the appropriate rocks. I wasn't *that* enthusiastic myself.

This a.m. I timed the downhill walk from cave to creek, a hair over five minutes; the upward journey takes two minutes longer. Any more than seven minutes of scrambling upward could be called strenuous, especially in that heat. Today I crossed the creek and, following a gully, headed in the direction of an interesting canyon roughly paralleling the one I inhabited. Within five minutes I stumbled upon centuries-old Indian ruins so dilapidated that the fallen walls were half-buried in the hillside. Even the pottery remnants had been reduced to one small fragment. Found myself reflecting on the joys and tribulations of those Native Americans (Hohokam, the vanished ones, perhaps?) who had lived in this secluded canyon so very long

Full moon Monday, May 22nd

ago. Doubtless they had sought shade in the very same cave that has given me coolness. *Requiescat in pace,* I murmured by way of a sincere salutation.

Midges maddening. Could do nothing about them except flap the bandanna around neck and face — and curse profanely. I passed through a stand — nay, a forest — of teddy bear cholla and stepped gingerly until clear of it. Though the spiked joints don't jump at passers-by as the popular name jumping cholla suggests, nonetheless they do cling steadfastly at the slightest touch or brushing contact. The spines, each one sharper than any needle, pierce the flesh at various angles and their removal (by means of a comb) is excruciating.

Having come through the cholla unscathed, I was attracted to a promising cave, so up the slope I toiled only to find that it was more of a rock chimney than a suitable dwelling. Skirting the base of the butte and with a wary eye on the downhill side, I came finally to a cavernous opening, partially blocked by a massive rockfall, the original cave-in. Working a way around it and entering cautiously, I heard fluttering movements and tiny squeaks. I stood in a bat-cavern and its occupants, furry as mice and managing to hang upside down and squirm simultaneously, did not appreciate my daytime intrusion. Nervously they flew to and fro, from this crack to that crevice, but not one out of fifty made a dash for the readily-available outdoors. Heavens, they might not have been gatecrashed like that for æons. Expected to be splash-bombed with guano, but they spared me. The place stank, it whined with mosquitoes, and I wasn't welcome, so, after a brief belfry-observation, I slithered off down the slope. Made the dry arroyo without mishap.

By this time, geographically, I stood directly behind a ship's-funnel-shaped butte which my cave overlooked — and what a classic canyon I'd rambled into. Its ages-worn walls rose sheer, and the geologic formations they encompassed were astounding in their sculptural diversity: amphitheatres (resounding with nothing but the music of the desert and filled with standing saguaros, not sitting people), windowrocks (through which peered the blue eye of the sky), human profiles chipped in rock, pharaohs' heads gazing imperiously over a desert not Egyptian, and towering cathedrals with spires, parapets, and buttresses built by Nature to house her desert gods. As if in greeting, the eternal silence of this inconceivably ancient sanctuary was pierced by the thin shriek of a red-tailed hawk as he sat preening himself at the top of a slender pinnacle. So saluting, he took to wing and swooped down, reddish tail seeming translucent in the shimmering sunshine. Then, as if to confirm the welcome (so I would like to think) the sweet tumbling song of the canyon wren, which so rarely shows itself, rang out pure and clear.

Though I did see a brackish pool, there was no spring in this roadless canyon; yet if there had been, I might never have wanted to leave it. More flowering golden-rain palo verdes on this side of the butte than on mine; on such a delectable density of blooms the bees buzzed — beside themselves with pleasure. Several large hackberry trees flourishing along the wash, too; by rooting there they benefited from the channeled floodwater whenever there was measurable rain.

Hiking back over the ridge with the distinctive outcropping of rock, I nipped an inch or so of a mormon tea (*Ephedra*) plant and chewed on it for refreshment. Oddly, it belongs to the pine family, has no leaves, is relished by livestock and, when brewed, makes a palatable drink. Supposedly it produces the drug ephedrine and was used by the pioneers to treat syphilis — how effectively I know not.

Took my pre-noon dip at the pool, throwing the tadpoles once more into momentary panic. Socks malodorous, needed washing, which I did. Back at the cave by shade-time. Tugged off boots, slipped on gym shoes and long trousers (anti-gnat procedure), and ate lunch of mashed sardines, green onions, garlic, cheese leftovers, and one boiled egg (t'other went bad on me, alas). From the kitchen to the study for more journal-writing until stretch-break at 3 p.m. when I made a swift trip down the hill and across to investigate sun- bleached bones I'd espied from the verandah. Came back with a solid, whitened, clean cow skull which I ferreted away behind a rock — for future collection?

Tomorrow morning will mark the fifth full day without setting eyes on another human being. It is unusual (and difficult) in this day and age to be able to be removed from human contact, by choice, for that long a period. I heartily recommend the experience, especially in a wilderness setting. Not everybody's cup of tea, of course, but decidedly mine. I've reaffirmed to myself what I've always believed: that aloneness is not synonymous with loneliness. I've discovered that I cannot, at this stage, totally eradicate irrational, primæval fears from my mind but that I can cope with them satisfactorily. Likewise rational ones. It is, for example, rational and certainly sensible to be afraid of being bitten by a rattlesnake (however unlikely) or of breaking a limb and being at the mercy of fate (much more likely) — but, to fear that a cave thousands of years in the making will collapse on one's head during the night or that a mountain lion will enter that same cave in the small hours and maul the sleeping human occupant, is simply irrational. And yet those atavistic fears keep worming their ways into the thoughts and must repeatedly be driven out by a twinning of twentieth-century commonsense and that finest of all antidotes to fear, faith.

Contrary to widely-held belief, not one creature of Nature's making is out to "get" man specifically. Take our friend the rattlesnake, for instance. The venom of that basically peace-loving reptile which unfortunately brings out the killer instinct in most men has been designed for hunting small prey and for self-defence — not, as mankind believes, for deliberate and hateful injection into human bloodstreams. The problem is reversed: it is, in truth, man who is out to get Nature. If this were not so, he could not bring himself to indulge, as he does so vindictively, in the gouging of the earth, in the destroying of minor habitats and major ecosystems, and in the polluting of the vital elements. It is not just man's brutality that angers me but more the fact that I happen to have an abiding love for Nature's works (in particular the Great Sonoran Desert) — therefore, it is unendurable for me to see that which I love being daily mutilated. Nature — or Mother Earth — is a most durable, dependable lady in my eyes; her affairs, being well-ordered, in balance and mainly harmonious, interest me considerably more than those of men, which tend to be fragmented and discordant. Furthermore for me Nature is the ultimate reality, a life-force that is truly tangible, a power that is perennial. To put it lightly yet lovingly, she has the knowledge to lift my head into the clouds and to keep my feet on the ground, all at once. In my backpack I carry this passage from *Tales of Power*, by Carlos Castañeda; it moves me deeply:

> This is the predilection of two warriors, he said. This earth, this world. For a warrior there can be no greater love. Only if one loves this earth with unbending passion can one release one's sadness, Don Juan said. A warrior is always joyful because his love is unalterable and his beloved, the earth, embraces him and bestows upon him inconceivable gifts. The sadness belongs only to those who hate the very thing that gives shelter to their beings. Don Juan again caressed the ground with tenderness. This lovely being, which is alive to its last recesses and understands every feeling, soothed me, it cured me of my pains, and finally, when I had fully understood my love for it, it taught me freedom.

Love cannot flourish without respect. So until people can learn to respect the earth, they will hold no love for it. Perhaps first and foremost they should learn to respect and love themselves as individuals and as a nation — and the loving and cherishing of Nature would be a matter of course, then.

Saturday May 20th 1978

Thunder, lightning, and a few drops of rain during the night. The cave was almost put to the dryness test. The storm never materialised and by morning the sky was clear again. I was up at 6 a.m. and for an hour and a quarter busied myself in packing and cleaning up the cave. Went through it with a fine-tooth comb for scraps of paper, dead matches, candle drippings. Filled in the fire and latrine pits in such a way as to leave no trace of their use. Decided to leave a dated note of greeting to anyone who might discover this cliff shelter; the note will probably remain unread till its author returns. By 7:35 a.m. I had gathered up the crushed beer cans, filled my water-canteen (and belly) and had set foot on the path homewards. Didn't meet up with anyone on the way out but did notice fresh bootprints several miles distant from the canyon. Highlight of the trek out was spotting two red-tailed hawks perched atop saguaros at quite a distance from each other; they were calling — or rather screaming — to one another and looked impressively large even from afar.

My Luvmobile, tucked away behind a mesquite grove, was untouched and in good starting order with all four tyres firm. I was back to base, safe, sound, and profoundly thankful for a grand experience.

II: Hombre de la Cueva: Second Cave Experience

Tuesday July 17th to Sunday July 22nd 1979

First Day

The trek began uneventfully. In the mid-afternoon I had been dropped off at the starting point and, grateful for cloud-cover, I set off at a regular pace. The rucksack, though heavy with a five-day supply of food, sat well on me. For the second year running I had it in mind to live as a part-time troglodyte, and my destination, complete with cave (different from last year), was already picked out. Trudging along, I saw a red-ripe saguaro fruit fall from its spiny pinnacle but, clambering down a slope to the base of the giant cactus, failed to find it. The Mexicans call this fruit (and that of the organ pipe cactus) *pitahaya*. It is deliciously sweet. Obviously a coyote, passing the same way, was in total agreement, for its fresh scat was made up of nothing but hundreds of the purple-black seeds of several *pitahayas*.

By late afternoon thunderheads had formed in the sky, and there began a great rumbling aloft. A summer storm rapidly moved across the heavens. Soon, accompanied by vivid flashes of forked lightning, the rain fell, gently at first and then in slanting sheets. For a while I didn't bother to take shelter, rather enjoying the coolness of rain so long overdue; but I came to an old and spreading ash whose canopy of thickly-leafed branches seemed to have been created especially for the wet wayfarer. There I waited till the downpour slackened — and drank from the close-by creek.

I pressed on, needful of reaching my cave before dark. Rounding a bend and glancing up at the mountainside to my left, I was stopped dead in my tracks by a fearful sight — *fire!* Just moments before the sun-desiccated brittle brush had been ignited by a spear of lightning and, because the rain had ceased, was blazing unchecked. The reddish-orange flames, goaded by a brisk wind, leapt up the flanks of the mountain alongside the one to which I was heading. The rampaging wildfire, greedily engulfing all in its path, made dreadful, crackling, snapping, whooshing sounds. I was horrified. It occurred to me that the appetites of both fire and man are much the same: Feed them and they will both grow; starve them and they will both die.

I was first on the scene — and found myself in a disturbing dilemma. Should I turn about, do a forced march to civilization and notify the authorities? Should I hasten up the hill and put

---

Provisions & Equipment for Six-Day Cave Experience Tuesday July 17th to Sunday July 22nd 1979

FOOD
5 carrots
5 nectarines
4 apples
2 oranges
2 onions
2 cloves garlic
12oz bread rolls
1/4lb margarine
3/4lb longhorn cheese
1lb brown rice
1lb lentils
1lb granola
1/2lb brown sugar
soy sauce, salt, pepper
loose coffee & tea
dried milk
orange drink powder
3 (8oz) cans pineapple
5 (3-3/4oz) cans sardines
chewing gum

EQUIPMENT
sleeping bag
foam underpad
small pillow
eating utensils
2 saucepans (1 lid)
1 plastic pail
1 gallon water jug
tennis shoes
spare pr. shorts
spare T-shirt
towel
medical kit
mosquito coils
5 candles
plastic cup
firegrill
plastic sack
paperback books
notepad & pen
soap, toothbrushes
shoulder satchel

out the lesser flames? Or should I make for the cave at a slowtop speed, being weighted down with provisions and water, stay put, and let Nature deal with this fiery outbreak? It was already dusk, and a dull, grey one at that, and there would scarcely be time or light to retrace my steps over the miles. Unshouldering my pack, I started up the slope toward the fires but then halted, quickly realizing the futility of my solitary action.

A plane droned directly above but held straight on its course, the pilot seemingly incurious. Surely he would radio to Phoenix and report the fire, I thought. A larger plane flew by but showed no visible interest. And then, to my vast relief, one half-hour after I'd first seen the fire, an official-looking helicopter hove into view, whack-whacked around and above the site for a while, and finally put down on flat ground below the moving phalanx of fire. What a burden off my mind and conscience.

Daylight was running out. With alarming constancy, horizontal and vertical streaks of jagged lightning rent the leaden sky, and the muggy air resounded with great shattering peals of thunder. I kept looking at the gluttonous fire and praying for more rain. It came, thank God, not too heavily but enough to discourage the flames. Nature, at her own pace, began to contain the blaze. Meanwhile, I was on the last lap of the journey, labouring and panting up the long incline to the escarpment at whose base lay my cave. Rain and sweat intermingled and dripped off me; the going was gruelling.

It struck me, as I inched up the slippery slope, that with a metal-frame backpack I'd make a choice target for a shaft of lightning, but I was feeling too tired — and too elated about the rain — to be frightened by that possibility. At seven o'clock on the dot, I pitched forward into the dry, dusty cave, gasping but full of gratitude. It was a while before I could bring myself to get organized.

Regrettably, a pair of canyon wrens whose rocky retreat I had invaded did not consider me welcome, and flew out into the twilight twittering plaintively. Their wall-nest had a fledgling in it but, happily, the young bird was able to take flight too. This relieved me because I doubted that the parent birds could've dealt with my intrusion. Felt badly about dispossessing them.

Just before dark I skirted the base of the cliff and reached a promontory from where I could clearly see the scorched mountainside. Only four patches of fire lingered on, no more than flickering pinpoints on a blackened background. The blaze had run its course. My sleep would not now be disrupted by a sense of dread. As it happened, it was utterly ruined by an onslaught of resident insects. Having cooked a late supper of rice, lentils, and sardines over a small pit fire near the cave mouth, I smoothed out a sleeping space, brushed aside the twigs, thorns, and pebbles, and laid out my bedroll in hopes of a sound sleep. It was, in fact, a miserable night, with scarcely a wink of sleep. Ants launched the opening attack. Those dealt with, I was then set upon by sand fleas and the blood-sucking cone-nose kiss bugs. The latter, not widely recognized, are surreptitious creatures that thrive in the summertime and are nocturnal; they first anæsthetize their victim (usually sleeping) and then draw blood, leaving their calling card, a hard welt. The cave was alive with them, adults and young. In the early hours, I lit a mosquito coil. This deterred some of the pests. I was glad to see the dawn come.

Second Day

The fledgling canyon wren returned at first light. It fluttered in and out of the wall crevices and stuck limpet-like to the soft rock. I lay perfectly still. The bird surprised me by all of a sudden flying at me and onto the pillow within inches of my left ear. Leaving a dropping on the pillow (a gesture of defiance — or derision?), it flew outside to feather-embrace the new day. Looking around, I noticed another resident, a black widow spider. She'd woven her untidy, sprawling web into the V-archway above the cave entrance. I watched closely as, with her luminous black legs, she gathered up her round, white egg cocoon and drew it behind her into the concealment of a crack. I'd no reason to interrupt the rhythm of her life. Secure in the knowledge that she was no night roamer, I knew she would restrict her activities to the confines of the formless web. An attitude of mutual respect, I should say.

For breakfast, an orange and a brew of black tea. The morning hike took me to the water-hole (where I dipped in the cold, soothing rock-pool) and then along the course of the creek to its confluence with another. Walking down a stony path, I saw out of the corner of my eye a hasty movement almost underfoot, heard a suggestion of that familiar heart-stopping sound, and caught sight of a coontail diamond-back rattlesnake disappearing into a bush. He didn't make himself entirely invisible, however. A length of his tail tipped with a yellow rattle was left dangling over a smooth rock. Though I had failed to spot him at a safe distance, he behaved in a discreet and gentlemanly fashion. He offered me no harm nor did he even threaten it. I thanked him for his tact and peaceful intentions — and continued on my way.

Not five minutes later I was boulder-hopping up the creek when another briefest of rattles sounded. There, on a stretch of cool sand, lay a black-tailed rattlesnake, not coiled in a striking position nor rattling — but merely with a wary eye on me. I sat slowly down on a rock. On sensing my goodwill towards it, the snake relaxed straightway and then, after a moment's reptilian reflection, glided off toward the bank in a calm and dignified manner. The markings of the black-tail, a higher-elevation species, are more pronounced and strikingly yellow than a desert coontail's. They are said to be of a docile nature. My own experiences with them surely confirm that. The muscle control of all snakes is a marvel to behold: They move with the litheness of a ballet dancer. They are worthy, beneficial creatures, sadly misunderstood, feared and hated without real cause, and wickedly abused by mankind.

This year has been uncommonly good for the blossoming of agaves (century plants); presumably the copious rains at the beginning of the year had much to do with that. Returning to the cave and plodding up the *bajada* in the late a.m., I passed a stand of them with their tall, sky-reaching stalks crowned with the glorious yellow and orange blossoms. No sooner have they flowered than they die. Their moment of triumph is their moment of death. I unwittingly flushed a ground-nesting poorwill, and there on the bare ground sat two pale-pink eggs, like a pair of exquisite oval pearls. Not even a crude nest enfolded them. What dangerous exposure to any predator wandering by. What folly. Yet there must be a method in it.

After a lunch of oily cheese, bread, and apple, I sat in the shaded cave (which is ten feet deep and five feet both wide and high) and concentrated for half the afternoon on writing up this account. For company I had scores of bee-like flies (or fly-like bees) which clung to the walls of the cave and buzzed furiously when agitated. Not bothering me, they were welcome. Now and then a curious hummingbird, attracted perhaps by the red colour of the plastic pail, came to hover at the mouth of the cave. Already the ants have become an unceasing nuisance; if there's a morsel of food anywhere they'll find it and throng the area. I've moved the perishable food all over the cave interior but the ants can locate it in no time. The most ant-free spot is in the middle of a jojoba bush growing at the cave entrance; there I balance the bag of food until the sun strikes it in the mid-afternoon.

The cave faces west toward a mesa vertically furrowed by bush-dotted dry washes. Later in the day, owing to this exposure, the intense afternoon sun creeps half-way back into the interior but, luckily, the corner in which I sit stays forever in shade. At half-past five this evening I lit a cooking fire and put rice and lentils on to boil. Despite sitting in shade I sweated profusely from the heat of both fire and sun. As far as I can see, no fires, ancient or recent, have ever been made in this cave — nor is there any sign of human occupancy, prehistoric or modern. Modern man customarily leaves some particles of trash, ancient man potsherds or smoke-blackened ceilings. Dried dung indicates that animals have stayed here — but am I the only *Homo sapiens* ever to do so? Could it be that previous passers-by were put off by the crumbling, friable nature of the chalk out of which my cave has been wind-carved over the æons? Even a scampering lizard will dislodge fragments from the roof, yet it appears safe enough to me. (The protruding knobs, ledges, and shelves I've put to good storage use.)

Nonetheless, as regards sleeping, I was driven from the cliff-dwelling by the conenose bugs, the midges, and the ants. After their tormenting on the first night, I moved outdoors and made a bed up on the level ground beneath the cliff, "just around the corner." Adequate overhang there to protect me from high wind and possibly some rain. Though there were two more black widows nesting in a shallow grotto, they were by no means hanging in my face and so were not part of the insect problem. I chose this spot because, although in the open air, it was a level space free from thick foliage, cracks, or crevices, and far enough away from any food source.

It happened, too, that I had a grandstand view of the electrical storm which, at nightfall, flickered magically above the brooding mesa to the north. Of fresh air I had abundance. Though insects did seek me out and nibble from time to time, I slept better out than in and wouldn't have woken up at one a.m. had rain not started to sprinkle on me. Prepared for that, I had by me a roomy plastic sack which, slitting down one side, I draped entirely over my bedding. Such anti-drenching measures weren't put to a severe test as the weather show soon ended.

Third Day

First thing this a.m., lurking within inches of my bedroll there was a conenose. Judging by the welts risen on my left arm, it had gorged itself on blood during the night. I had no compunction in killing it, a messy business, with my own blood splattering the rocks.

By 9 a.m. I was trotting downhill to the spring. An attempted shortcut became a bushwhacking affair; the descent took twenty-five minutes. Last year's cave also stood at the head of a slope but much shorter than this one, with water only seven minutes away. Yet this climb was healthy for me, the exercise vigorous. Reaching the pool, shaded and kept cold by the broad branches of sycamores, I threw off my clothes and sat squarely down in the clear, clean, cool water. It washed away the tiredness, the grime of the cave, the stinging of the insect bites, and the sour sweat of overheatedness.

Springwater of the wilderness seems to revitalize not only the tired body but the life-weary spirit itself; in one's nakedness, it renders one innocent again. It evokes the long-suppressed joy of childhood. It brings one, as nothing else can, into intimate closeness with the soul-core of Nature. It is a baptizing.

This creek, bone-dry in places, then trickling wet through light-green mats of algae, I followed for several miles. It cut between two high and sun-parched ridges and, wide and wandering to begin with, it narrowed as the mountains pressed in on it. I came upon sylvan pools that hosted tiny aquatic life: orange-spotted beetles, timid tadpoles, and fully-grown frogs, water boatmen that rowed beneath the surface, minnows darting frenziedly to and fro.

After two hours of leisurely hiking, I chanced upon a long-forgotten cabin site by which grew a fig tree, laden with ripening fruit. Planted years ago, presumably, it'd been left to fend for itself. A floodwall, overgrown with lichens of various hues, still stood sturdily but of the homestead itself nothing remained. Was it a miner's place? More than likely, for there were precious few Thoreaus in those southwestern days of yore.

Returning, I crossed paths with a slim garter snake wriggling in a shallow pool, a pair of racers which slithered off into the bushes upon sensing me, a flycatching black phœbe, a nesting dove that flew twittering in alarm from its rough lattice of twigs in a willow — and a collared lizard, a most colourful reptile with a light-green body, a ring of black around its neck, and red epaulettes. The collared is not frequently seen.

Surprised myself by getting back to the spring in just over an hour. Before tackling the long hill, I took a soap bath. So as not to pollute the pellucid water, I had first to immerse myself and then stand free of the pool, soaping and scrubbing. The rinsing-off was done with pailfuls of water scooped out of the creek, one at a time. This system of ablutions worked, and I was thoroughly clean. Trying for another shortcut, I climbed a game-trail up the bank and was walking by a prickly pear cactus when I saw, wedged in it, a sun-bleached bull's skull, perfectly intact. I yanked it half-way out — and let go as if it were red-hot. Yellowjackets had built a nest inside this skull and were vexed at being molested. One zoomed out and stung me on the right elbow. I beat a retreat, bearing a sharp pain with me but glad to have escaped with just one sting. One day, when the wasps have moved on, I'll retrieve that classic skull. Today's only other casualty was poor Horace, a shepherd's crook I brought over from England. I rolled a boulder in the creek bed; it fell on Horace's only leg, shortening it by six inches. *Mea culpa!*

Back at the cave by 2 p.m., overdue for midday lunch, and ravenous. In the afternoon I worked on this journal for three hours. Made a culinary variation this evening by melting slices of old cheese on top of the rice and lentils, this instead of sardines. Result? A viscous mess that looked worse after adding soy sauce but had a fair taste to it. With a Japanese dinner staple of fish and rice, I've cut the overall weight of the backpack: the net weight of a can of sardines is 3-3/4 oz., whereas a can of the favoured beef stew is 1 lb., 8 oz, or 15 oz. at the least. As to rice, one pound of it lasts quite a while.

Retired to my cliff-ledge after eating, unravelled myself on the bedroll and listened to the special sounds that come with twilight and the night. A canyon wren, perched on an outcropping, gave out its last cadent call of the day, a sweet series of falling notes, each as clear as a bell. Down below by the meandering, mesquite-fringed creek, a bull bellowed in that mournful way. In the darkening sky close to the cliff the bats silently appeared, fluttering and swooping through the air in a ceaseless effort to take their fierce fill of night insects. Each one of the myriads they were snapping up meant one less potential assailant of me. Bats, the great devourers of mosquitoes, are always a welcome sight.

I lay on my back for a long time gazing up at the stars, now and then glimpsing a fast-falling one. To the north again was an illumination of sporadic lightning, without the bombast of thunder, with no sound and fury reaching my ears. As the jagged lightning-lit clouds moved towards me, I took the precaution of slipping underneath the plastic sack; but not a drop of rain fell all night long and I slept fairly well.

Fourth Day

A young scorpion was crawling about this morning. I gathered it up with a handful of dirt and flung it down the slope. It wasn't the painful species, *Centruroides sculpturatus*. The morning was overcast and cool, one of misty melancholy — superb hiking weather provided the rain held off. Buzzing around a jojoba bush below my ledge was a squadron of bright yellow and black bumblebees. Their purpose eluded me.

A liquid breakfast, a cupful of orange drink. Leaving the cave before 9 a.m., I reconnoitered the base of the cliffs in the hope of finding other hideaways. No luck, but I did come across a sumac (sugarbush) bearing ripe berries. They have an acid-sweet taste with a large seed and an edible casing and were relished by the former native peoples and early pioneers.

Dropped down the talus slope to the creek and once more indulged in the luxury of soap bathing. The clouded sky and a cool breeze made it a colder procedure than yesterday's, but nonetheless refreshing. I filled the gallon and half-gallon containers with fresh water and, under drizzling rain, set off up the hill. From my marker it took exactly a quarter-hour of upward slopework to arrive at the cave. By now the least-steep route had been established. Warily passing by the prized bull-skull, I noted it to be still tenanted by yellowjackets and kept on my way. Further along, on the desert floor, lay a scattering of potsherds, fragments of clay jugs used centuries ago by prehistoric peoples; they were plain pieces, without design and of burnt orange colour.

Being by myself, I have this week partaken freely of fresh garlic. This lunchtime was no exception. If it be true that garlic issues from the skin's pores, then I hope the local insects will like my flavour less.

At midday a low bank of raincloud fell upon the rim of the mesa, hiding its line of agaves and junipers from my view. Yet still no downpour. Lately there'd been much blustering by the climate but precious little action. "Full of sound and fury signifying nothing," as Will S. put it. After lunch I made the discovery that the upstairs apartment — the rock cleft above and to the left of the cavemouth — was lived in by a colony of wild bees. Standing outside, I heard a deep, muted droning above. Upon climbing around a jutting rock, located the hive and watched the animated comings and goings of its owners. Earlier, within a stone's throw of the bed-ledge, I'd seen a long-vacated grey and empty honeycomb built into a cliff-recess.

I've succeeded in ousting my fellow man from this venture of solitary refinement in every way but one: aeronautically. This region, wilderness per se, is still close enough to the city to be overcrowded with 'plane traffic. Only minutes ago, a helicopter whacked noisily overhead, its mechanism making such a din that it might just as well have been landing on the cave roof. No doubt it was on a worthy mission looking out for wildfire but, even so, it shattered the natural tranquillity of the desert and detracted from my feeling of isolation. 'Copters are a blessing when you need them and a curse when you don't.

The mid-afternoon being cooler than usual, I chose to roam around for an hour or so. Ahead of me a roadrunner dashed off in a flurry of spindly legs and flapping wings, and I counted that sighting of the desert's jester-bird as a good omen. The ramble took me up a fairly steep slope to the craggy end of a hog's back ridge. There I sat and reflected upon the gloomy gloriousness of the day and on Nature's verdant vista that encompassed me. I contemplated my great fortune at being where I was. And at having the good health and state of mind that made it possible. I gave thanks.

After a time my roving eyes began to discern a certain symmetry to a group of rocks beyond and above me — it *had* to be the work of man. My reverie came to an end; I jumped to my feet and hiked swiftly up the spine of the hog's back toward this surprise objective. Guessing it to be an extensive and well-preserved Indian ruin, I pressed upwards with growing excitement and soon gained the wind-whipped heights. I stood on the threshold of what once must have been a fortress-community. Owing to its lofty location hundreds of feet high, it could never have been attacked — or even attained stealthily — without extreme difficulty. It had been constructed on the flat top of a mountain which fell away sheerly on all sides — not as awesome an edifice as, say, the Hopi pueblo of Walpi but still impressive.

I entered by way of an antechamber whose walls on one side stood solidly at six feet. Stepping over fallen sections filled with rubble, I edged by two smaller rooms, neither of which was roofed. If *vigas*, roofing timbers, had originally been used, there was no longer a trace of them. The walls that still stood were at least three feet thick, some built with two outer layers of slabrock and then packed, sandwich-like, with loose stones and heavy gravel. At the far end of the bluff stretched a wall ten paces along the cliff-edge; it rose to eye-level, perhaps five and a half feet, and nowhere less than chest-high. I pace-measured the length and breadth of the confined plateau on which the ruins sat. It was fifty feet long and, in the widest part, no more than twenty. Here and there in the earth lay a few potsherds but no other artifacts at all. A fire-circle, the inevitable bits and pieces of trash, and a graven inscription (LM.DJ May 5th 1953) on the face of a boulder proved that this stern sanctuary was not unknown to the whiteman.

The major part of the ruin was choked with desert chaparral. Below, on a wide saddle, had been an extension of this community for I could make out more dilapidated walls. No springs up this high, so one could imagine the toil in carrying water to the heights from the canyon far below. In this remote place I disturbed no one but a hawk perched on what must've been his favourite rock for it was white with guano. With a thin scream of protest, he took to wing over the abyss. I felt privileged to have stumbled upon this ancient habitation and, on leaving, I murmured my salute to the spirits of those long-vanished peoples, perhaps the Anasazi. How I envied them the intimate knowing of this desert land before "civilization" came with its dams and dikes, its severe overgrazing, its powerlines and strip mines, its mutilated mountains, its throwaway beer cans.

Scrambling up the slope to the cave, my eye fell upon two earthenware fragments, one of them six by four inches. The previous belief that early man had never used this cave began to sound incorrect and, within an hour, I was to be proven wrong. I was sitting on the dirt step a few feet back from the mouth peering outside (and, with ample water, shelter, and food, feeling secure in a primæval sense) when I spotted an unusually smooth piece of granite jutting out from the soil by the cave opening. An inquisitive tug at it revealed a slightly chipped but well-formed *mano*. Someone *had* shared the same rocky roof hundreds of years ago. A *mano*, Spanish for *hand*, was the stone implement used for grinding corn, beans, and seeds on a bigger concave rock (known as a *metate*) in the mortar-and-pestle principle. This *mano* was slim, fitting the palm well and measuring about six inches long by three wide. The acquisitive side of me whispered, "Take it! Keep it!", but upon reflection I left it in the cave where it belonged, carefully hidden and with a fair chance of being left alone for the rest of time. For me the thrill was in the finding, not in the removing.

This evening I boiled another batch of rice but skipped the lentils. The sardines I served up separately too, having mashed them up with chopped onion and garlic. This meal had a little more class to it — if caves and class can ever be said to go together. The fire was temperamental. At one point smoke billowed out of the cave-mouth, which annoyed me, not wishing to have the attention of passing planes. I didn't want "rescuing" in mid-experience. Brewed up a saucepanful of cowboy coffee, sat back and did some more black widow watching.

Most of the time she'd leave her cocoon suspended, outside and in plain view, from a fine silken thread. There, at the whim of the air currents, it would gently spin, first one way, then the other. On occasions, maybe anxiety-ridden, the spider widow would grasp her white egg casing and hurry with it deep inside the fissure. Like all other venomous animals, she is quite innocuous unless threatened or mishandled. The primary goal of this spider, marked with a red hour-glass on her belly, is to produce more of her kind — not, as too many would have it, to live for the moment when she can inject neurotoxin into the veins of mankind.

Fifth Day

A hummingbird, ever curious, kept flying into the doorspace to peek at me in disbelief and to thrust its long, whiplike tongue out at the red pail. Given its diminutive size, that tongue must surely be the longest on earth. Another unexpected visitor this a.m. was an orange dragonfly which flitted twice up to the widow's web, enquiringly. A pair of lizards paid a call, too, and the male didn't hesitate to display to me his vivid turquoise underbelly and inflated dewlap — all very macho, just like his show of power with the pushups.

The morning's roamabout began early. By 8:30 I was sliding down the slope. Went exploring another way today and, thanks to the gentler contours, the hiking was less strenuous. I encountered more Indian ruins in an open, accessible area but all the walls had tumbled down. After yesterday, an anti-climax. From there I side-trekked a quarter-mile or so to the head of a ravine which, at a distance, held promise of a hidden spring. It took a bit of bushwhacking to get to the spot but all was dry as a biscuit there. Not a fruitless jaunt, however, for, as I topped a rise, there in front of me, twenty-five paces away at most, stood a young mule deer. Our surprise at running into each other was, I'm sure, mutual. She stayed motionless for a few instants and then, with great ears pricked up, cantered off through the chaparral in elegant leaps and bounds, halted once — briefly — to look back at me (incredulously?) and then disappeared over the brow of a hill. What a delightful encounter. It was altogether a very pleasant day-hike. I saw some wild edibles ready for the harvesting: the hackberries, orange in colour and sweet, grew plentiful and ripe. Plentiful too were the twisted seedpods of the cat-claw acacia and the beans of the palo verde (green stick). Both could be ground into flour and eaten as a mush. Once in a while my boots would brush against rattleweed which, with its seeds loose in their casings, made a disconcerting sound. On occasion, when daydreaming, I sprang back defensively on hearing it.

Two hours of uncomplicated hiking carried me to a spring in an arroyo and there, appropriately, I soaped, rinsed, and bathed myself. The limpid pool was being busily frequented by yellowjackets but they came in a drinking not a warring mood. And so, with interest, I was able to study the manner in which they landed on the water's surface and skimmed over it without soaking their bodies or wings. In essence, they used their legs as light pontoons — fascinating.

Turned about at this stage and got back to the cave in time for lunch. Along the way there was more coyote scat full of the seeds of the saguaro fruit. It must be the special of the month on their July menu. They've neither howled nor yelped at all this trip — not within my earshot, at least. I've missed their singing, as the Mexicans call it. But perhaps the summer is not the season for it.

Wrote up this narrative in the cool of the cave during the afternoon. Having committed myself to keeping an account of this "cavexperience," I cannot neglect it — though it becomes onerous at times. Before the light failed, I read a few chapters of *The Inheritors*, by William Golding, author of *Lord of the Flies* and *The Spire*. Then to the sleeping shelf in time for a dinner performance by the other black widow, making short work of a black beetle caught squirming in her web. At first she appeared to play with her hapless victim, as a cat does. I'd never before seen a black widow dealing with her captured prey. Sleep was slow in coming, perhaps because I knew that the conenoses had found my night retreat and were poised to bite. Five of them never lived to see the following morning.

From down in the lowlands came a loud but harmonious chirruping and trilling of crickets. Above me, in the glittering heavens, there would suddenly appear — and just as quickly vanish — a brush-stroke of white light which I guessed to be the tail of a comet. And also man's satellites weaving their ways through the unnumbered stars.

Sixth & Final Day

The morning of departure — already. I restored the cave to its original state, filled in the fire-pit and removed all traces of my presence save a sheet of notepaper on which was written

To the next occupant of this cave — greetings! From Tuesday July 17th to Sunday July 22nd 1979, I stayed here and apart from the biting insects of night, enjoyed the solitary experience. If you arrive before the end of the second millenium (2000 a.d.) send me a postcard or write a note at the foot of the page.

Yours, Geoffrey Platts, [address], U.S.A.

I left a ballpen. A month or a millenium could pass before another soul takes up residence here. I may stop by again myself one of these years. Who knows?

"Fare thee well," I said gratefully to the mountain that had sheltered me; "Adieu!" I bid the widows and the second-floor bees, and even the ants and conenoses. And on my way I went downhill, homeward. I watered for the last time at the creek and, under a flawless blue sky and penetrating sun, I set off at a steady pace over familiar terrain. It was my intention to reach the halfway point before midday and rest up during the hottest hours at a spot that I knew held water and shade trees.

Following a wash I spotted in the sand a curious insect, more common south of the border than in Arizona, a dung-beetle. Characteristically, this one was pushing its ball of dung o'er hill and dale and working earnestly at what to human watchers is rather a comical task. Interestingly, it uses its four rear legs to propel the ball and is itself moving backwards all the time. They are scarab beetles, considered sacred in ancient Egypt and known as *mayates* in Sonora, Mexico. This one was plain black — the Sonoran variety is iridescent green.

On the odd prickly pear, a prolific grower in overgrazed areas, there were *tunas*, the purple fruit. Because it seemed too early for them to be ripe, I sliced one open. Ripe enough. As a rule, these edible cactus fruits are harvested in September. I noticed, too, that dodder, that peculiar parasite, had thickly entwined its orange tentacles around several acacia bushes.

An hour before noon, I arrived at the midway spot. Having made good time, I could look forward to five hours of rest and refreshment. In the ample shade of a massive, leaning granite boulder, I settled back to enjoy the tranquillity. At 3 o'clock I had been on this trek for a full five days without setting eyes on a single human being. Minutes later I heard voices. Upon this quiet place, with raucous cries of delight, descended a family of day-hikers. Goodbye, sweet solitude. Hello, everyday world. I gathered up my baggage and slipped away unnoticed. So ended my second cave experience.

Though there may be risks attached to camping, hiking, and cave-dwelling alone, the rewards far outweigh them — in particular for those who cherish and need their moments of solitary refinement.

> And lifting up mine eyes,
> I found myself alone,
> And in a land of sand and thorns.
>
> — Tennyson, "Holy Grail"

Love thy desert
Here come those developers again Geoff!
Ask not what your desert can do for ye— ask what ye can do for your desert!
Carl 91

III: Siete Salidas del Sol: Seven Sunrises

July 25th to August 1st 1980

First Day

The summer sun rose on the first leg of my seven day foot-journey. Even at the height of summer, though, the desert-day starts coolly — and I was capitalizing on that. It was cool underfoot, too, for I had to wade along a lovely flowing creek whose bed-sand was reddish and whose banks were lined with the riparian "big five:" sycamore, cottonwood, willow, ash, and walnut trees. The early morning sun touched the crowns of the towering cottonwoods and their light-greenness became suddenly luminous. The birds bristled into activity with the fresh energy that each sunrise brings to all life. I saw large hawks soaring above the tree canopy, then a troop of crows that wheeled about the cliffs and cawed in protest at the sudden sight of a desert wayfarer splashing his way down the shallow creek that no doubt marked their territory. A flash of red in the creekside foliage had me thinking "Cardinal!" But, no, a closer look showed me a summer tanager with its yellow beak, scarlet body, and brown wings.

In places the canyon walls glowed salmon-pink. It was these walls that, after ages of endless erosion, had formed the red bed of sand through which I trudged. This pink, the egg-shell-blue of the summer sky, the soft green hues of the trees, and the trailing wild grapevines blended beautifully into a colourful whole. It was a sight to soothe any city-ravaged soul. At times the cottonwood seedlings grew so prolific along my stream path that I had to side-step so as not to crush them. So many cottonwood and sycamore seeds germinate — only to be scoured out by the flash-floods of summer. Always that balance in Nature, so hard to attain in our own lives.

A little way above the stream habitat stretched dry desert-slopes, some forested with many-armed giant cactuses whose spiny extremities were punctuated with the crimson *pitahaya* fruit, opening in four-petalled fashion to expose a black core of thousands of tiny seeds. This fruit of the saguaro is relished by all desert creatures, myself included. Later, along the trail, I saw coyote scat composed of little else.

Sooner than expected I came upon the creek's confluence with the solitary river. Rested a while and at this point filled a gallon plastic jug with water in anticipation of the scorched desert ahead of me. Eight more pounds of deadweight to be

---

Provisions & Equipment for a seven-day footjourney July 25th to August 1st 1980

FOOD
7 carrots
7 oranges
3 apples
dried figs
1 clove garlic
8oz dried potatoes
1.5-lb loaf of bread
1/2lb margarine
5 cups brown rice
2lbs granola
1lb brown sugar
8pkgs dried soup
1 small can of beans
4 cans of sardines
3 cans of devilled ham
1 small can of beef stew
dried milk
loose coffee, tea
peppermint gum
condiments

EQUIPMENT
sleeping bag
foam underpad
small pillow
eating utensils
2 saucepans
water jugs (1.5 galls.)
candles
firegrill
50ft cord
tennis shoes
spare T-shirt
towel
2prs spare socks
light sweater
novel
notepaper & pens
toothbrush etc.
shoulder satchel
Instamatic camera
monocular

carried — but in a parched climate there is no living alternative. Old Sol had ascended rapidly and from now on the going would get hot. With a week's supply of food, the backpack was not light and, toiling up the broken trail in the brassy glare of a July sun, I became more and more aware of the water-weight's burden.

Sad to say, this wild stretch still carried the messy mark of man, chiefly because of accessibility to off-road vehicles. The beer-barbarians had of course left their trail of cans and bottles — a visual blot on this lovely, lonely land. In a fit of anger I thrashed a Coors can with my walking stick and cursed the despoilers of the desert. Calming down, I gave myself over to listening to desert sounds — the discordant chatter of a cactus wren, the persistent *wheet-wheet* of a curve-billed thrasher, the forlorn *coo-coo-coo* of a mourning dove, the buzzing of busy worker bees, the sighing of a breeze in the sultry stillness of noon when all life except the shrill cicadas quietens in the sweltering heat.

The map had already helped me pick out a campsite. Though knowing nothing of the terrain, I was assured of river water. Now and then the cool river down below would come into sight of the high trail but there was no scrambling down those cliffs for a dip. Tantalizing indeed. By eleven a.m. I swore to myself that in the days to come I would be done with hiking long before this hour — even if it meant rising before daybreak. Half an hour later, sweat pouring off me and shoulders aching from the leaden weight of the pack, I came to the river's edge. Ah, what a joy, what an incomparable relief to plunge naked into that glorious river! I wallowed there like a hippopotamus while the day's aches and pains dissolved into the moving waters. Refreshed and restored, I then set about shifting my baggage to a near-island in the middle of the wide, mostly dry river bed. There, a leaning willow gave latticed shade and there was a mirrored, still backwater close by. And, for fire-making, an abundance of driftwood.

"At home once more, safe and sound," I thought. "Let tomorrow take care of itself." The noonday meal was a devilled ham sandwich laced with fresh garlic, an apple, a handful of home-dried figs — all this washed down with a cup of mint tea.

I spent the afternoon writing this journal, resting up, and watching thunderheads rallying in the sky, and, at one point, a great blue heron lazily flapping its way through the warm air above the winding river. Later, taking advantage of an overcast sky, I forded the river (waist deep but slow-moving) and reconnoitered the opposite bank in hopes of finding the trail continuation. I was lucky and did locate the trailhead, marked by a cairn. As a rule I don't favour these man-built pyramids of stones but several times today I was grateful for their existence. There was no sign of recent foot travel in these parts — which pleased me. Returning down an incline I slipped on loose gravel and was spared a disagreeable drop over a rock shelf by a low shrub which I grabbed.

Eyeing the thunderheads, I debated whether to move the tent across to the other river-bank — but decided on staying put and having faith in an absence of flooding overnight. Bobcat pawmarks pricked the otherwise-pristine sandbanks bordering the river. I did see a man in the distance at the water's edge. Felt a twinge of annoyance at the realization that I wasn't totally alone. Before dark, I padded up and down the smooth yielding sand feeling its texture between my toes; stroked by a river breeze and surrounded by beauty, I was glad to be where I was — free and unencumbered. I went to bed at nightfall but the atmosphere hung heavy and hot and, in spite of being tired, sleep was slow in coming. Shortly after eleven p.m. a rainstorm fell upon the tent, which billowed like the sails on a tea-clipper. Wind! Thunder! Lightning! Rain! Much excitement for an hour and then, at midnight, a fading away. The tent held up and I stayed dry.

Second Day

An enormous Colorado River toad greeted me first thing as I crawled bleary-eyed out of the tent at five a.m. I didn't sleep soundly but a dip in the pool brought me awake rapidly. The tent had almost dried off and my pack, covered with a plastic bag, was dry. The rain had sweetened the air: it was fragrant, greenery-damp, invigorating. By six a.m. I was packed and ready to ford the river which, mercifully, had not risen during the night.

Balancing the pack on my head and shoulders, I cautiously entered the water and eased my way across, foot-feeling ahead of me for submerged obstacles. Made it! Went back again for the lighter baggage and noticed that the water, at its deepest, came up to my navel. I thanked the river and *Madrecita,* Mother Nature, for a safe crossing. Taking a shortcut up the cliffside, I picked up the trail without difficulty. The sunrise was accentuated by the ragged dark clouds persisting in the eastern sky after last night's squall. As the walking remained cool and level for the first hour or so, I was able to enjoy the vast untrammelled surroundings. Redrock bluffs plunged precipitously down to the riverside and afar off, yet prominent, I could clearly make out a butte shaped much like a woman's breast.

It struck me, as I hiked, that I wasn't about to starve along this expanse of Sonoran desert for, bordering the path, grew jojoba bushes laden with ripening nuts, pencil chollas with plump but prickly orange fruits, occasionally sweet hackberries, and the odd prickly pear cactus with purple spiny *tunas* growing from its light-green pads. As I walked, I sampled, marvelling at the wild foods which this arid desert produces — and at the bountifulness of Nature. These things made for a superb morning. I felt the joyousness of Walt Whitman when he wrote

> Afoot & light-hearted I take to the open road, healthy, free, the world before me, the long, brown path before me, leading wherever I choose.

Gambel's quail, whirring away from me and twittering in alarm, and cottontail rabbits, bolting from their hiding places, were my frequent companions on the shining start of this new day. Shed antlers, bleached by the sun, told me this was deer country too. Crossing washes, I noted the sacred datura, a toxic plant once used by Indian shamans to induce visions, displaying its showy, trumpet-like moonflowers; yellow-blooming devil's claw too and a scattering of remarkably-late desert marigolds.

For perhaps a mile the trail ran high above the twisting sweep of the river, then wound down to river-level and meandered confusingly through a mesquite *bosque*, the floor of which was dead grass, the colour of flax, beaten down by the recent rain. It was an enchanted arbour roofed in completely and full of singing birds. Since mesquites have been chopped down as firewood by Indian, Mexican, and Anglo alike for a number of centuries, these *bosques* are now few and far between. Emerging from this wood into open desert, I thought, "How wonderfully wild this country is! May it never be tamed by man."

After an hour and three-quarters of steady hiking, the path dropped down again and passed by a cove cut out of the riverbank. I took time to explore it and was so entranced by this spot that I decided to make camp and while away the entire day and night there. It'd been a brief hiking day but then yesterday had been long and arduous — and I was on this walk to experience its solitary pleasures, not to break long-distance records. The cove had a soft-sand beach that gently sloped into an eddying backwater. Around it fragile damsel-flies with colorations of turquoise, scarlet, and royal blue flitted playfully. One sole cottonwood up on the bank provided shade. A smaller willow, half-uprooted, made an ideal clothesline, camp seat, and hat peg. The view upriver and all about was outstanding.

My first visitor, a racer snake, lost no time in slithering under a tree root, followed closely by the zebra-tailed lizards specially color-adapted to the beige sand-dunes (dotted with the pale-purple deadly nightshades). Here, within sight of my cove, the river formed an oxbow impressive to the eye.

I pitched the tent, dug a firepit, collected wood, and made the site liveable. By nine a.m. I was off on a stroll upriver. How wide the bed was — at a guess, a hundred yards in some places. For a while I kept to the broad banks but then began to walk in the very middle of the great swath cut over the millenia by the eternal river. Being low season the water was flowing in one narrow channel, but flowing vigorously. Up against the cliffside I chanced upon two interesting phenomena: a massive sycamore trunk completely hollowed out and yet nevertheless supporting two tall and healthy limbs in full leaf. They were literally growing out from no more than a bark shell. And a spring cascading out of the bank about a dozen feet above the river level. From where it issued forth was a young ash tree whose roots had been bared by the force of this freshwater fountain. The ground above it was dry. The water seemed to gush out of the very bowels of the earth. I drank from it gratefully. Across the river, midway up the cliffs, a black-mouthed cave caught my attention. Curious, I swam the channel and picked my way carefully up the loose rock slope through defiant stands of teddybear cholla. It disappointed me to find a beer can near the mouth of the cave but there were compensations in the form of potsherds, half of a broken *mano* (pestle), and a pair of tiny corncobs less than two inches long, left by Indians centuries ago. The cave was spacious but it stank of guano. A glance up at the shadowy roof showed a cluster of bats hanging and squirming together.

Back down on the flatland there was *Pepsis*, the black and orange tarantula hawk-wasp, searching avidly for a great hairy spider which she would paralyze with her sting, drag off to an earth-burrow, and then lay eggs upon it. The hatched larvae would then feed off the still-living body of the wretched tarantula. Other members of the wasp family, the venomous yellow-jackets, were doing their thing too — landing lightly on the surface of the water and floating downstream with the current until presumably they'd had enough to drink — or enough joyriding.

I wandered back to the cove and prepared a lunch of sardines, chopped garlic, bread, apple, and dried figs. Sitting in the shade of the waterside willow and eating my food, I gazed fascinated at the water slipping by. And I remembered the passage in Herman Hesse's *Siddhartha*:

> The river is everywhere at the same time — at the source and at the mouth, at the waterfall, at the ferry, at the current, in the ocean and in the mountains, everywhere. The present only exists for it, not the shadow of the past, nor the shadow of the future. The secret to be learned from the river is that there is no such thing as time.

During the summers of 1978 and 1979 I sought solitude in caves and wrote accounts of both experiences. Two cherished friends expressed the desire to have known more of my feelings, thoughts, and reactions on being absolutely alone for a prolonged period, something which few people have had the chance or inclination to do. Upon reflection, I must say that not only am I used to solitude but that I embrace it like a lover.

Therefore I am neither bored nor threatened by it. On the contrary, it brings me much peace and pleasure. Undeniably, however, having over the past five years come to terms with the shadow-side of myself, I would be more prone to value a state of solitariness. When one has finally made this inner compromise, so vital to the spirit's well-being, there is nothing any more to fear from the opportunity to think, which naturally comes with solitude. By and large, modern living contrives with every possible excuse and distraction to avoid confrontation with the inward self. Meaningful musings are not encouraged by society and so a healthy wish for aloneness by those who want and need to think is viewed as suspect.

Though this explanation may appear cryptic and perhaps baffling to those who do not know me well, I can say with certainty that my stretches of solitary refinement have brought one paradoxical truth to my consciousness — that the worst thing that ever happened to me proved to be the best thing for me.

Close to the cove was a rock bay attracting deep waters and there, smoothly swimming just below the surface, was a pair of fish a foot or more in length. I guessed them to be bass. At twilight I lay back on the giving sand and watched bats dart out from their cliffrock shelters and begin their fluttering forage for insects. Since being able to observe a colony of bats at roost, I've grown to care for them more. Like snakes, they arouse an unjustified abhorrence in people of the West — yet in old China a bat was a symbol of happiness. While taking a dip as night was falling, I had a dozen of them twisting and turning, whirling and swooping about my head — as they snapped up insects within inches of the water. Nearby a nighthawk performed similar maneuvers; no wonder it bears the dialectic name of bullbat.

I was about to retire for the night when, on turning around, I was startled to see a huge silver disk rising in the vee of the canyon behind me. It was the moon. And it was one night short of being full. Though the night was clear, it didn't cool off. I slept only fitfully, unclothed on top of the covers.

Third Day

There were still stars in the sky when I got up at 4:45 a.m. but within twenty minutes it was daybreak. I slipped into the river to wake myself up and, doing without a cup of hot tea, managed to be on my way by half-past five. Summer hiking demands a dawn start — only mad dogs and Englishmen are still on the move after 9 a.m. I looked back at the cove — a prettier spot one could hardly have imagined.

Fifteen minutes after setting out, the thought that I hadn't yet encountered a rattlesnake popped into my mind. Then, sure enough, as I rounded a bend, there was a western diamond-back, dusty and dull-coloured with its striking coontail. It lay straight across my path ten yards away so I stopped and waited, respectfully. It kept a sharp eye on me but it wasn't until I made a slight move that it began rattling and took up a semi-coiled posture. I said in a gentle voice that I was a friend, not an enemy — but this didn't reassure it and it crawled away into the bushes. I was fascinated to observe that it could actually "walk back-wards" or, more explicitly, was able to retreat with its head twisted around to face me uninterruptedly. The perfect defen-sive withdrawal. I took our meeting to be a good omen.

The sun broke through the light cloud-cover and lit up the uppermost half of the great breast butte, brightening the redness of its sheer cliffs. Shakespeare put it more poetically in one of his sonnets (33):

> Full many a glorious morning have I seen
> Flatter the mountain-tops with sovereign eye

Kissing with golden face the meadows green
Gilding pale streams with heavenly alchemy.

Suddenly I saw movement out of the corner of my eye. I stopped in my tracks. There in the brush trotted a desert fox, the size of a small dog, several yards to my right. It stared at me, nervous and mesmerized, but because I stood motionless it held its ground and didn't dash off. A beautiful animal. Its fur was mainly grey with patches of russet around the neck and by the ears, which were pricked up. Its eyes seemed slanted and with them it looked me over for threatening behaviour but, seeing none, lost interest. Even when I moved on, it stayed where it was. Ah, Zorro, it was a privilege to cross paths with you.

Once more the trail left the desert heights and twisted downwards to the river banks, then vanished. There was deep water and a slick-faced cliff where, according to the map, the trail should've led. I had no choice but to ford the river twice in order to regain the trail. Three successive years of high water must have wiped out this part of the trail. All was well, however, and I did find my way back onto the straight and narrow. This pathfinding was proving to be a useful experience for me, particularly as the trail was not always well-defined, causing me to wander off the not-so beaten track from time to time. Basic commonsense was involved, for the original trailblazers had, understandably, followed the easiest contours of the land. This meant looking over the terrain now and then and putting myself in their position as planners. A map and the rock-cairns especially were a great help, of course. Criss-crossing by cattle, a washout or an overgrowth of weeds often caused a temporary loss of trail. Nothing more than Nature reclaiming her own.

After a steep ascent away from the river which had made a wide sweep, I came down to the lowlands again and passed through a larger mesquite *bosque*. It was more mysterious than the first, spreading over several acres. My footsteps made no sound for I was treading on soft earth carpeted with rain-flattened grass. By eight o'clock, just as the sun was gaining strength, I'd reached the end of a day's journey. It was at a major confluence of waters, where river joined river, a merging of life-forces. For a campsite I chose a shaded nook beneath a bent willow whose tangled roots drew water from the placid river. Not done with walking for the day, I set down the leaden weight of the backpack, took stick, cap, and satchel, and did some scouting upriver. The purpose was to locate the beginning of the upland trail for the next stage. Doing this saved a good deal of unnecessary exertion at the time of departure. I did find what I was seeking — but not before some sweaty sidetracking.

Stumbled upon an old line-shack used by cowboys at round-up time in the fork of two converging canyons. And also extensive Indian ruins where, strewn about, were brownish-orange potsherds and even an oblong *mano* for grinding seeds and grains. Even more intriguing to me was the fresh spoor of what had to be a mountain lion on a wind-smoothed sand dune. The paw-marks were impressive — scarcely smaller than my own hand, fingers splayed. It had come down from the mountain to drink at night, I imagined.

I returned for lunch, seeing with dismay that my paradise was polluted. On the opposite shore there were three piles of trash left, I supposed, by thoughtless floaters or boaters who passed this way when the river was up.

After cooling off in the pure waters of the confluence, I lay in the shade of a mesquite out of the glare of the midday sun and wrote up this journal. There were two distractions from the duty of writing: the sight of a zebra-tail lizard pursuing and devouring a grasshopper. And that of a pair of great blue herons flying low over the water. They made an unmusical croaking sound, odd enough to startle me. In mid-afternoon rainclouds masked the sun, letting me hike up the merging river for a mile or so. Here, on a rocky sandbar, I spotted three foxes which at first I took to be coyotes. But they were scrawnier and much redder. When I softly whistled at the last of the trio away, he halted and looked back at me, curious.

Yet more great blue herons. I've seen more of these elegant birds in the last few days than in my whole lifetime. They're keen of vision and take to flight even at a long-distance glimpse of me. In spite of the resonant rumblings and the glowering clouds, only a few drops of rain fell. Much ado about nothing.

On the way back I passed the ruins of a long-abandoned cabin. The only distinguishable thing left was an ornate potbellied iron stove, rusted and in many broken pieces. A dark shape in the water looked familiar and I stooped down to briefly pick up a turtle with pretty hexagonal markings on its algae-stained shell.

Supper over with, I sprawled out in the sand to watch the liquid motion, the eternal passing of the river. And there were fish breaking the surface to feed on insects. During the night I heard loud splashes that suggested a fish of Moby Dick proportions — and also bizarre noises that I could not identify, only guess at. They came booming from across the water, sonorous sounds rather like a cross between the bellowing of cattle and a foghorn. What else could it have been but some gigantic bullfrog?

Fourth Day

This confluence campsite was too special a place to leave in a hurry — so I stayed put. At 6:30 I was off on a side trip upriver, carrying sandwiches and a camera. The river meandered like a serpent but, as it kept wide, I'd no trouble in staying alongside.

There were times when I'd shortcut through mesquite and hackberry thickets and, in doing so, twice met up with diamondbacks. One curled up fast asleep was too drowsy to even rattle hello and the other was slender and motionless, its mouth open and eyelids closed, revealing nothing more than a tiny slit. It did close its mouth before I walked on, but behaved as peaceably as the first one. *Gentlemanly* is the word for the many rattlesnakes that I've run across on roamabouts; in no way are they deserving of their reputation for meanness. So often it's man who is the vicious one.

Shortcutting through the riparian underbrush turned out to be often more trouble than it was worth. For I never came out of it without lacerations from cat-claw acacia, the so-called "wait-a-minute" bush. Above, on the hillsides, the agave century plants — with their deep orange blossoms filled with nectar as sweet as honey — gorgeously bloomed and died, simultaneously. Reaching the second confluence, my morning's destination, I drank from a fourth source of fresh water in as many days. Pasted to a corner cliff-face were the bulbous mud nests of white-throated swifts. These birds, the daytime equivalent of bats, swooped and soared, snatching insects from the air. In the deep where rock ledges slanted into the water I got a dim glimpse of two shoals of perhaps a dozen fish each. They weren't living in fear of the hook and line along this reach where men and machines could not trespass.

Ah, how thankful I was, too, to be beyond the range of those infernal machines, their damaging tyre-tracks and the garbage that inevitably follows in their wake. It was here that I did something I'd never dreamed of doing before. I found beer cans littering a grassy bank and tossed them into the flowing river. Rather than let them remain on the banks forever, I made the reluctant decision to return them to man by way of the river. They would end up as an ingredient of that filthy soup which accumulates at Horseshoe Dam — man getting his own back, as it were.

I ate lunch beside a clear pool under the spreading branches of an ash. I was overwhelmed at the knowledge of my good fortune and richness at being in such a tranquil spot. I've never felt freer than I have on this trek, a strange, almost primordial feeling, like the awe of being First Man.

Set off back to camp at eleven a.m. when the sun was high but, being lightly loaded and close to the water all the way, there was no hardship from the heat. Now and again I'd immerse myself, shorts, shirt, and all, and continue on naturally air-conditioned.

Back at two o'clock, I brewed a pot of tea and wrote a little until raindrops made me put away pen and paper. As with the day before, however, the black clouds were dispersed by the sun. At nightfall I went down to the confluence and again studied the bats in flight. What tremendous energy they put so silently into their nightly business of feeding. They appeared to me as whirling dervishes of the air. Yet I made every effort to rid myself of the last lingering fears — instilled by legend and superstition — and sat unmoving on a waterside boulder while they fluttered around my face and head.

The bellowing in the bushes started up again after dark and went on resonantly, mystifyingly, throughout the night. It sounded as if it were being amplified in an echo chamber. One day someone will solve that enigma of the river for me.

Fifth Day

Slept in till six o'clock and then made tea over a mesquite fire whose coals and smoke gave off the distinctive aroma of that hardy desert tree. The mesquite's deep-reaching taproot can go down more than fifty feet into the earth. It is said that dying ones are an indicator of a lowering of the water table. Much like the presence of ironwoods, mesquites denote frost-free pockets in the winter desert.

This day was set aside for rest and reflection with nothing more strenuous than a stroll or two. I started on one such stroll through the *bosque* at the back of me and, as I was entering the thicker part of it, thought I heard voices up ahead. Not ready for my privacy to be shattered, I back-tracked, crossed the creek, and sat down in a cool place to do some writing. Returning later, I could see no sign of people in the open but, upon penetrating the wood a short way, I caught sight of a red tent between the trees and heard a boy's voice. Time to move on. It was too late in the morning to attempt serious hiking, so I compromised by shifting camp to the line-shack up above the river, a half-hour away. In this manner I got myself away from the too-closeness of the unexpected backpackers and also put half the steep hill behind me.

This new stopping place had running water, a pool deep enough for bathing, a tin roof against the rain if I should need it, and a panoramic view of the mountains and buttes sliding down at sharp angles to the wide shores of the river below. By a stroke of topographical luck I was actually able to see the former campsite in the distance. The disagreeable aspect of this rancher's hut was the collection of years of rubbish all around it. I considered filing a litter complaint against the cattlemen who obviously still used this structure set on public land. In the air was a fragrant piney whiff of juniper; I knew from these evergreen trees that the altitude lay between 3,000 and 3,500 feet, which would mean cooler sleeping than at river level.

Looming above me were four colossal rock buttresses with perpendicular dropoffs to the boulder-clogged gullies below. I rolled out the foam pad and sleeping bag on an iron bedstead beneath a gnarled mesquite, intending to spend a night under the stars if neither rain nor insects fell upon me. Walked back down to the river to wash my hair, a shirt, and bandanna, and, after toiling up the slope again, took a dip in the creek-pool hemmed in by the contorted, flood-bared roots of a cottonwood tree. Almost unconsciously I started to play like a carefree little lad, undamming and clearing a waterway choked with leaves and branches. I was quite naked. The thought came to me that a wilderness experience such as this was one of the few ways left to us to recover, however momentarily, a measure of our lost childhood innocence. It often seems to me that we can only truly be ourselves in the exclusive presence of Mother Nature and, knowing her to be unjudging and impartial, we can at last let go and give ourselves utterly to the moment — as young children do.

Frequently on this walk I've caught my mind reverting to the past or anticipating the future (for example, the reunion with my ladylove). And so in order not to lose the essence of the present happenings, have willed my mind to return with fullest concentration to the "immediate here and timeless now." This being-here-now, this intense involvement in the present moment, so very hard to attain in a culture either hooked to the past or hellbent for the future, is an ongoing, unrelenting discipline. Without it, though, there can be no harmony.

More rumblings and grumblings from overhead in the afternoon. A shiny black-crested flycatcher let out several single-note peeps as if in protest at these disturbances aloft. But again no rainfall and in the early evening the westering sun pierced the clouds, allowing me to take a picture of the line-shack. My home for a day.

Customary dinner of brown rice and cream of chicken soup (dehydrated). In case of a night-time downpour I stored all kit in the hut and while doing so flushed a canyon wren sheltering in the rafters. Suspended from the ceiling by thin wire was an old coffee can on the rim of which was precariously built an amazing nest of mud balls and twigs. It was unoccupied and didn't seem to belong to the wren tenant. After tying down the sleeping bag, I climbed onto the creaking springs of the rusting bedstead and spent a comfortable night in the open, fanned by a gentle down-canyon breeze and harassed by no insects at all. My sense of well-being was completed by the rising of the moon over this place of rest.

Sixth Day

I rose with the birds to beat the heat again. Before setting off, I wrote this note for the owners of the line-shack: "This is such a beautiful canyon. Why do you treat it like a trash dump?" For two taxing hours I slogged upwards, farther and farther away from the river, my unfailing water source. As I trudged steadily higher the stands of juniper thickened and the giant saguaros were left behind. Agaves, yuccas, sotols, scrub oak, and prickly pears took their places. No rattlesnakes greeted me this morning but I did come upon an odd little snake, no more than a foot long, with a black head and chequered markings. Later on, a five-foot bullsnake materialized before me, making me jump back instinctively. Their considerable size and their intricate body patterns of yellow and brown make them handsome reptiles.

Along the ascending track, in fact a rutted and disused road, I noticed the cloven hoofprints of deer, but their owner was nowhere to be seen. A red-tailed hawk, whose keenness of vision is legendary, screeched at me from afar but the climb was too punishing for me to pay it much attention. Of the four-footed animals I saw only cottontail rabbits — although I wanted to believe I found a pile of bear scat and claw marks on the trail. In all honesty, I cannot vouch for that, though.

The dryness of this land of juniper and jay birds was a problem. Luckily, I'd foreseen this and was lugging along a gallon and a half of drinking water, an extra twelve pounds. During the morning's three and a half hour hike, I passed by only one wet spot, a stock tank with a pool of brackish water the colour of pea soup. Not too appetizing. Though the sun was not as ferocious at this elevation, I thought it wisest at nine o'clock to conserve bodily water and rest up until evening under a shade tree. Looking off to the horizon I observed with distaste that the atmosphere was tainted even here in the wilds: a murky haze that, on a day as clear as this, could only have been smog borne aloft from the cities and the copper mines.

The sky got dark and gloomy. By three o'clock it was raining in earnest. I seized the opportunity to cover more miles (in hopes of finding a spring where I could drink, bathe, and make camp for the night) and set out still uphill, in driving rain. I decided not to care about getting soaked and to give myself entirely to the elemental — hiking bare-chested in a lively summer storm. My mouth was open wide with tongue thrust out to catch the wind-driven raindrops. And I sang a song of thanksgiving to Mother Nature on behalf of myself and the thirsty, cracked earth. Having never done it before, I dropped down on all fours and sucked from a rain puddle. Its muddiness or mineral content gave it a bitter taste. After the initial exuberance at giving myself body and soul to the deluge, I sobered up and thereafter found little joy in plodding up an endless gradient in sticky mud which clung in great gobs to both boots. Although this clodhopping up a slippery slope was no fun, I was still thankful for the cool respite that the rain had brought.

The only living creature I saw during this hour-long cloudburst was a jackrabbit bounding off through the chaparral. The skies then lightened, the rain stopped, and I began to dry out, looking for all the world like a mudlark. Still no springwater, only foul-looking liquid in stock tanks, so I kept pressing on at a slow but sure pace. In one hand I clutched Horace, my Yorkshire shepherd's crook, and in the other the jug of water on which I'd been sipping all day.

Two minor upsets had occurred earlier in the day: the strap had broken on a shoulder-satchel used for carrying maps, paper, and pens, odds and ends; and, worse, melted margarine had dripped all over the food bag. The mess was indescribable. Little of my equipment escaped the grease. Fortunately this didn't happen until the latter part of the trek.

At six o'clock I gave up on finding freshwater and, very footsore and weary after nearly seven hours of actual hiking, collapsed under an ancient alligator juniper beneath which lay the only patch of level rock-free ground for miles. Seven o'clock came before I could stir myself to prepare food — and I was ravenous. Rain hadn't fallen on this particular area (which made pitching a tent more pleasant), but it did do so in the night for just a short spell. Glad to be within a half-day's walk of the journey's end, I slept soundly.

Seventh Day

I stayed in my sleeping bag an hour later than usual. There was no urgent need for a start at the crack of dawn, especially as I'd climbed to an altitude (about 5,000 feet) where the morning sun was much less fierce. This campsite was set in the middle of a field of sunflowers though it was still too early in the year for a mass of rich yellow blossoms. Just a few here and there. The trail, no more than a furrowed farm-track, wended toward the east, so I assumed that I was on course. Heading into the rising sun across open grassland, I was besieged by armies of grasshoppers leaping wildly, left, right, and center. Dropping down into a shallow valley, I came upon the first pine trees. These tall and proud ponderosas, straight as shipmasts, symbolized the end of the road for me. They were not only a welcome sight but a scented reminder of halcyon days in Yellowstone and Yosemite. The river, my refreshing companion for five full days, now lay 4,000 feet below. I thought it odd that the low-lying desert, sweltering under a summer sun, should have more sources of clear water than these pine uplands. One often fantasized countless creeks trickling through meadow and forest. Perhaps, though, I had chosen the driest trail in all of the high country.

For three hours I pressed on through the pines, keeping to a deserted ranch-road that seemed to wander at will. My water was nearly finished but at this point it wasn't a matter of concern — even though the day was hot — because I knew it wasn't far to a faucet. At half past ten, turning a bend in the red-earth backroad, I looked down from the mesa and saw civilization several hundred feet below. I was home free! And twenty hours ahead of schedule.

Public land changed to private, so I hid my baggage behind an obliging clump of manzanita bushes and ambled down into the small Arizona town. Here I filled up the water containers, posted a letter, stopped in at a country cafe to buy an apple, tomato, and a fistful of Hershey bars, and then plodded back uphill to the campsite on the public side of the boundary line. It was, I reflected, just as well that I'd reached my destination a day early because I did need rest before reuniting with my friend.

After catching up on this diary, I rambled around the immediate area examining the unfamiliar highland plants. Not all the flora looked strange to me. I recognized the ochre-barked manzanita and its edible berries, the short spruces reminiscent of pale blue Christmas trees, the hairy "lemonade-berry" relative of the sumac, big oaks with twisted knotty limbs, the upright horsetails growing in flat, moist ground and used by the pioneers as panscourers, the live shrub oaks with acorns still green, and even the striking red Indian paintbrushes which came and went with spring in the desert.

I was careful with the cooking fire, clearing a circle down to bare earth and digging out a keyhole-shaped pit with a pointed stick. I felt that the private residents a stone's throw away (but out of sight) might smell smoke and come running. Happily this didn't happen; my privacy remained intact. The pinewood gave a pleasing aroma and burned well. The last of my food was prepared and I was pleased with the way the week's menu had been planned. At dusk I took a lazy stroll along the red road into the forest. I should've been exhausted by rights but, not in the mood for sleep straight after dark, I read a chapter or two (by flashlight) of that magnificent 1937 novel, *The Rains Came*, by Louis Bromfield. It rained before midnight but not heavily or for long.

Eighth & Final Day

The sun beat on the tent's screen door and brought me out of a deep slumber at 6:45. My last morning — and the first day of August. I was slated for a reunion at the bottom of the hill in the little town. Time? High noon. Place? The general store. There was no haste around camp on this morning, no sense of urgency to be on the trail before the heat of the day. The dead coals in the Indian pitfire I pounded into a black dust, covered it with earth, stamped that down, and then scattered the pine-needle duff over the entire surface. I unstaked and lowered the tent and then tossed branches and pine-cones over the flattened space it had sat on. I gathered up what bits and pieces of old trash there were. The result of these little labours of love was a forest floor restored to its natural state. When the time came to leave there was no longer any sign of my having been there. As always, I took pride in that fact and yet, in truth, it was nothing more than an act of gratitude to Nature for her kindness and hospitality toward me. I did not forget to give thanks to the forest place itself, either.

The heart-warming reunion did take place on time. The foot journey was over. I had gone into the wilderness not as a conqueror but as a loving visitor; I came away from it not with spoils but with rich memories.

Estimated hours of hiking: 20.5, plus 10.5 hours for sidetrips, total: 31 hours.Estimated mileage of route (excluding sidetrips): 30 to 35 miles.

IV: Cañon Escondido: Hidden Canyon

First Day

Danger is often associated with solitary hiking — in fact, one is advised never to go out into the desert alone. I am aware of the risks involved (broken leg, snakebite, etc.), however, but choose to continue hiking solo — simply because total solitude (in the company of only God and Mother Nature) is for me one of life's great joys. And so, for the fourth year in a row, I found myself tramping off into the wilderness, deliberately seeking out a remote and roadless area. Even with the sun declining, the temperature was still clinging to the 100° F. mark. It wasn't long before I felt the dead weight of the backpack and the leaden tug of the hand-carried knapsack, full of oranges and canned food. Horace the Second came along for the experience, too. He's a Yorkshire shepherd's crook that my friends had recently brought over from England. It was his maiden voyage into the wilds.

For two hours I trudged an uphill course following a bone-dry arroyo. I consoled myself with the thought that the pack would be much lighter on the way back — for the food would be off my back and in my belly by then. Lizards skittered away from me as I plodded along the rocky wash. Once, I was startled by the sudden whirring of wings and chip-chipping of a covey of quail I'd flushed from the cover of a jojoba bush. Dusk turned to darkness as I rounded a great bend in the dry wash and came to the place where I was counting on water. With relief I saw the spring had not dried up and that, in spite of cattle-tracks, the water seemed clear and potable. And it was with sheer delight that, minutes later, I stripped off my T-shirt — sodden with sweat — and slipped naked into the shallow pool.

Provisions & Equipment for solo trek August 23rd to 29th 1981

FOOD
4 cups brown rice
2 lbs. granola
dried apples
fresh apples
6 oranges
pkg. carrots
2 cloves garlic
jalapeños (peppers)
chiltepines
1 lb. brown sugar
can devilled ham
can potted meat
2 doz. tortillas
5 sm. cans sardines
3 sm. cans pineapple
6 pkgs. dried soup
5 bouillon cubes
2 pkgs. noodles
10 boiled eggs
lemonade crystals
salt
English snuff

EQUIPMENT
tent
sleeping bag
small pillow
foam pad
hunting knife
can opener
knife, spoon
plastic drinking mug
lg. saucepan
2 gallon water containers
spare socks & T shirt
light pullover
knapsack & satchel
length of cord
plastic bowl
candles
snakebite kit
hand soap
shampoo
detergent liquid
toothbrush, etc.
2 plastic sacks
spare comb
paperbacks
notepaper
matches, lighter
watch

Those aching limbs were soothed by the cold blessed water and the cuts and scratches from catclaw and scrub oak washed clean. Such a moment was a dream come true for a desert roamer.

Because of the lateness in setting up camp, I ate a cold supper of tortillas and sardines—though, afterwards, I did stew up a bowl of dried apples and brew a cup of cowboy coffee. The Milky Way and a skyful of glittering stars, some of them shooting across the heavens, seduced me into sleeping in the open without a tent. No sounds — save those of a skunk rustling in the bushes and a summer choir of crickets — broke the stillness of the night. No rain fell nor did any ants or conenose kiss bugs bother me as I slept. The night was utterly peaceful.

Second Day

I believe that I am now in my second childhood — not (I hope!) in the senility sense of the phrase but, rather, in the literal meaning. When I was a boy, my grandfather felt that I should be a naturalist, for most of the summer days of my boyhood were spent happily, carefreely wandering in the woods and along the hedgerows of the English countryside. (There was no television in those days, thank God.) Then, in my late teens, I took to girls and pubs and forgot about the wonders of nature and the simple pleasures of rambling. The drinking, party-going, and philandering filled up all of my twenties and most of my thirties. Upon finally coming to my senses in the late thirties, I went back to the woods, or, more correctly, struck out into the great Sonoran desert. With this desert as my beloved friend and teacher, I've been as happy as a sandboy ever since. Yes, I have found my second childhood to be delightful. Nature (or, as I now call her, *Madrecita*, Little Mother) has become my everyday companion and, frankly, I much prefer her calm company to that of my fellow man in general. I have become disenchanted with the weak and wanton ways of man who is, for the most part, blinded to nature's beauty by his greed and crass materialism. Collectively he suffers from a sickness of the spirit; this is so obviously manifested by his destructiveness towards the Earth, the very thing that nurtures him and whose health is critical for his own survival.

> The world is too much with us, late and soon.
> Getting and spending, we lay waste our powers;
> Little we see in Nature that is ours;
> We have given our hearts away, a sordid boon.
>
> — William Wordsworth

The foraging skunk, with a broad snowy stripe running from the tip of its tail to the top of its head, had me propped up on my elbows at first light. It shuffled close to me, gave a long look, and then scampered off into the undergrowth. I dashed cold water on my face at the spring, ate an orange on the move, packed up, and lost no time in getting on my way. Onward and upward. In the sweltering summertime it is wise to take full advantage of the first few cool hours of early morning — especially when burdened like a burro. As usual I greeted the rising sun with a, *"¡Buenos dias, Sol!"* and just as its heat intensified I reached the divide and began a steep, slippery descent, helped greatly by Horace, who became a supportive extension of my right arm.

Here and there were signs of old fire damage, such as junipers burnt almost to charcoal, completely gutted. Dropping down slopes may take less energy than struggling and panting up them but it is more perilous because of the ever-present chance of slithering downwards head over heels. I got down safely, however, and followed a spectacular red sandstone gulch on its twisting, plunging course. At one point a fifteen-foot slick-rock slide had me lowering the lurching pack by rope to the base. By then I was heating up along with the sun and so was elated to come across water trickling from a side gully. Because of the desperate dryness of the season, this gave me heart. Further on there was more water and then some "trees of life," cottonwoods and sycamores. And so I knew that, provided I kept to this canyon, I would not suffer death by thirst.

In mid-morning, as my stamina was faltering, I caught sight of something I didn't want to see: a crude shelter of branches and twigs much like the old Apache wickiup. That in itself wasn't offensive; it was the rubbish inside and scattered outside, too. There were filthy blankets, cracked plastic containers, rain-soaked books and magazines, cigarette ends, aluminum foil, tobacco tins, and the other trash that blights our throwaway society. The camp had been lived in for a time but abandoned months ago. I undertook the task of restoring this pretty place beneath a large juniper to its former state of wilderness. Such a squalid mess seemed all the worse in this pristine, unpeopled stretch of wild land. Digging a deep pit in soft sand,

I threw in all the garbage. Using the books and magazines as combustibles, I made a blazing bonfire. After an hour or so of burning, I was able to tamp down the ashes and fill in the pit with loose earth. The shelter I tore down, spreading the branches around the area. This thorough cleanup took me most of the morning but I felt good upon accomplishing it, as though I'd paid my dues to Madrecita for this desert venture of mine. I thought of leaving a nasty note at the site in case the despoilers ever did return.

Ate a hearty lunch of boiled eggs and tortillas, washed down with a mugful of mint tea, and spent the better part of the afternoon writing up this account in the shade. During a break from scribbling, I took a brisk, breath-catching dip in a nearby pool and nibbled tart, blue-black wild grapes from the vine hanging over it.

Wanting to find my own special spot, I moved on in the late afternoon with a wary eye on the thunderheads gathering darkly in the east. The streambed along this stretch was mainly waterless and parched — though now and then there'd be a brackish pool or a patch of damp earth where wasps, bees, and butterflies were clustering. Stepping over one such sunken bowl of moist sand, I found myself in the midst of a cloud of small white-spotted orange butterflies. The growl of thunder and blackening sky persuaded me to pitch a fast camp. Choosing a high and flat piece of ground made spongy by a bed of juniper duff, I found firewood hurriedly and quickly put up the tent. Perfect timing! Because then drops of rain began to spatter on the nylon tent roof. More peals of thunder and lusty gusts of wind but, oddly, no downpour came and so I didn't fulfill a longstanding desire to see a wall of floodwater come crashing down a narrow canyon.

The evening's meal was interrupted by an errand of mercy — returning to the creek a live and frantic water-bug which I'd inadvertently scooped up and dumped in the coffee water. Twice this happened. I must confess that this Schweitzer-like "reverence for life" began to wear thin after the second time. I ate my fill of tortillas, sardines, and brown rice, crawled into the tent and, being too exhausted to read, lay down and drifted off to sleep.

Third Day

This endeavour to live life fully in the here and now — so much a part of my philosophy — is not something learned, acquired, and then forgotten. It is a daily, even moment-by-moment discipline. My Anglo-Saxon mind is so thoroughly trained and conditioned not to live in the present (but rather in the dead past or insubstantial future) that I am forever having to will my thoughts back to the Now. If I fail to do this and persist in, say, future-tripping, then my experience of that alone which is tangible — the infinite here and timeless now — becomes diminished. While preparing a fire for coffee yesterday, I willed myself into an acute awareness of what I was *actually doing* and became conscious even of the twigs being used for kindling: their feel and texture, their look and the brittle sound of their cracking and snapping. In that superb philosophical statement and final novel of his, *Island*, Aldous Huxley wrote:

> So be aware, aware in every context, at all times and whatever creditable or discreditable, pleasant or unpleasant you may be doing or suffering. This is the only genuine yoga, the only spiritual exercise worth practising.

I believe that most of us amble through life in our own tight and tiny worlds with scarcely any appreciativeness for the immediate and precious Now — or any true awareness of the acts we're carrying out or of the words that we say or that are said to us. We miss out massively, don't we?

This a.m. I slept in, having no heat to beat nor any campsite to find. Breakfast was an orange and coffee. Looking through the food bag, I found that some of the pre-boiled eggs had already gone rotten and hurled them far into the bushes. Down at the creek, naked as a nymph, I stood on a rock and poured cold water all over my sleepy body. This had me wide-awake in no time. Glancing up at the bluff above me, I counted no less than a baker's dozen of barrel cactuses growing sturdily out of rock-crevices. And at stream level grew tall yellow night-blooming primroses, wilting in the rays of the climbing sun.

A little later I was off (backpackless and therefore light-footedly) on a scouting side-hike. Keeping to the creekbed which broadened after a while, I was allowed a soaring view of the jagged, red-walled canyon towering on both sides. For safety's sake I carried with me a full gallon of drinking water. The sun rose higher in the pure-blue sky, the August heat pressed down on me. I caught a fleeting glimpse of a large, grey shape and heard the breaking of branches as it crashed through the chaparral on the bank. A javelina (collared peccary) perhaps? Then turning a boulder-strewn bend I saw the swift and sinuous movement of a Sonoran whipsnake as it too made a getaway. Most curious of all was the high-pitched whine that came from it in full flight.

I was about to set off again when I heard a light rattle and, to my excitement, spotted a pair of black-tailed rattlesnakes wrapped around each other. Since snakes are chiefly solitary creatures, these two had to be making love! The smaller one, which I took to be the female, had a stunted rattle and she, no doubt piqued at me for having disturbed their loveplay, withdrew to a shady nook 'neath a boulder — with the male pursuing her. I crept slowly to within six feet of them — and then stepped back sharply for she seemed to make an aggressive lunge and came part way out of the darkened hole. Was she really angry at my having disrupted a moment of rare reptilian rapture? Or was this forward move of hers just curiosity? No matter — this lissom lady was no longer eager to consummate her love with a human voyeur in the vicinity so she slithered out of the hole, wound her way upwards through a tangle of dead flood-jammed sticks, and vanished into a jumble of boulders on higher ground. As she slid away, the burnished gold diamond markings on her back expanded and contracted in a most fascinating way. The more placid male lingered a while and then with his forked black tongue flickering in and out also made his departure, though sluggishly. Earlier this year I was privileged to come across a courting couple of western diamond-back rattlesnakes ("coontails") who were far less concerned with my peeping presence than these two. It's profoundly sad that most humans will kill rattlers on sight. Those humans could learn so much by keeping their distance, staying still, and observing the snakes. Far better to relocate than to kill. That reverence for life again. Henry David Thoreau put it well:

> Every creature is better alive than dead — men, moose and pine trees — and he who understands it aright will rather preserve its life than destroy it.

Horace's clattering on a rock drove a great horned owl from his daytime cover in the shade of a sycamore and he flapped away to find a more peaceful place. Turning off up a side canyon and hiking over an arid stretch, I was at last gladdened by the sweet sound of a flowing creek and soon arrived at a small but inviting pool of clear water. Above it loomed a saguaro cactus of not only giant but gigantic proportions, a stately and truly magnificent specimen. Here, under a spreading ash, I rested, ate lunch, bathed (ah, bliss) and continued writing. An inquisitive hummingbird paid me a visit and so did a scarlet dragonfly whose "bi-plane" wings sparkled in the sunshine like tiny diamonds. In Mexico, dragonflies are called *caballitos del diablo* — little devil-horses — a picturesque name for them, surely.

From behind me came a thin, frantic squawk. There in the rocks a few yards away one of Nature's grimmer dramas was being enacted. A Sonoran whipsnake had seized a plump leopard frog by the hind leg and was dragging the wretched thing into its den. I have come upon this agonizing scene before and intervened on behalf of the frog and saved its life. But this time, accepting that the snake had to eat, I did not interfere — but did become witness to the whole devouring of the screaming yet oddly passive frog. Peering into the rock-crevice to where the snake had stopped for supper I could actually see the frog disappearing bit by bit into the widening jaws. The reptile, with deadly efficiency, worked its mouth gradually up the frog's back leg, then bit deeply into its rear end and kept methodically consuming until, at last, I saw the victim's head and bulging eyes vanish totally into that awful maw. The whipsnake then continued masticating (or was it smacking its lips?) and opening its black mouth wide every few moments. At last, as if drawing down the curtain on this gruesome drama, it sank out of sight down into that horrid hole. Perhaps only the slow death of a fly trapped in the web of a spider can be as terrifying as that of a frog in the deathgrip of a snake. Later on in the day, I was to see a great green grasshopper caught in the web of a desert funnel-spider, but its size and strength enabled it, after a tough struggle, to tear free from the sticky strands.

In the early evening, I retraced steps back to the tent. Being hot and tired, I slipped gratefully into the sunlit pool nearby. A scurrying movement in the gnarled, flood-bared roots of a creek-side tree drew my eye to a light-brown scorpion going about its business. It's not often that scorpions show themselves so openly, especially during daylight. This one paid me no heed nor I it.

More leaden skies at twilight, some far off thunder — but, again, no rain fell. Having got back to camp in good time, I had enough light to cook supper in a leisurely fashion. The burning juniper wood in the small Indian pit-fire gave off a distinctive and pleasing cedar aroma, yet the smoke did nothing to drive off the no-see-ums, tiny, nearly-invisible black flies that bite in the evening time. Once inside the tent I read by candlelight for a short while, but the heat generated by the twin flames got too uncomfortable to bear. So I put the candleholder (an oval sardine can) just outside the tent and through the insect screen watched the flames flickering and sputtering in the dark. They attracted the inevitable suicidal moths and, surprisingly, a large brown hairy tarantula who high-stepped around the campsite for several minutes. Primitive man's television. I floated off to sleep with the plaintive cry of the poorwill in my ears.

Fourth Day

> Give me the splendid silent sun with all his beams full-dazzling.
> — Walt Whitman

Certain of my friends are puzzled as to why I should want to roam about the desert in the notorious heat of the Arizona summer. Why not do your hiking in the cooler northern part of the state, they ask? Or why not do your solo desert trek in the wintertime? For me, it just wouldn't be the same. The desert comes into its own in mid-summer; it is at its most glorious because then all the marvellous heat-adapting systems of its fauna and flora are in full operating order — and taxed to their utmost. One glances, for example, at the sun-browned resurrection fern clinging tenaciously to the hillside earth and presumes it to be lifeless. Not so! It merely plays dead. At the first vigorous rainfall it will spring into vivid-green life and make an arid slope quite verdant. A miraculous performance and yet just one of many among desert dwellers. So, if the plants and animals of my beloved desert can make the best of their lives during the harsh heat of summer, then I would wish to, too. And, besides, at this torrid time of year, there are far fewer people out and about — which, being a solitary fellow, pleaseth me. It could even be said that Noel Coward had a point when he wrote that line, "Mad dogs and Englishmen go out in the midday sun."

This morning was given over to exploring minor arroyos and seeking out other waterholes. It is odd in the desert how some washes will start out as dry as dust and suddenly, when least expected, lead to lush oases where grows all manner of moisture-dependent vegetation. I've run into quite a few clumps of cattails this trip; they're elegant plants with many uses. I can never pass them by without thinking of the biblical story of Moses and the bulrushes. In our region, cattail pollen was most sacred to Apache medicine men.

This exploration took me high up and along a hog-back. I was rewarded for my sweating efforts by a superb desert vista of mighty proportions. My eyes swept over this silent panorama of crag and canyon, slopes and sky, boulders and bush, and, for an instant, imagining myself to be the only man on the face of this great Sonoran desert, I felt awed and filled with reverence. May this land remain inviolate, I prayed. May it be left in peace forever to fulfill its own natural destiny — without the grasping, destructive encroachments of mankind. "Long live the desert!" I shouted to the four winds.

Dropping down to the canyon bottom once more, I began to think of Colin Fletcher's marathon walk through the Grand Canyon and his description of it in *The Man Who Walked Through Time*. He spoke of hiking nude and of the sense of freedom from physical and social constraints by doing so. On a whim, I decided to emulate his experience and spent an hour rambling up a ravine wearing nothing but hiking boots and a satisfied smile. It must've made an extraordinary sight — bare bum, bollocks, and boots — but it did feel light and exhilarating. There is genital vulnerability, of course. One has to do an occasional cupping of hands in the lower regions when moving through cholla and cat-claw country. Furthermore, in the penetrating rays of the summer sun, one does incur the risk of the dreaded "three Ps" — pinkness of the posterior and the privates. All in all, though, I can highly recommend bare-bottomed bush-whacking to those footloose and fancyfree in the wilds.

I made my way back to camp in time for lunch. Having partaken of food, drink, and a dip, I settled down beneath a tree to read, write, and reflect. In this tranquil manner, I whiled away the sultry afternoon.

It was at dusk, as the light was failing, that *Madrecita* made me privy to one of her countless miracles. I'd just finished dousing myself with cold creek-water and drying off when an impulse led me over to the long-stemmed yellow primroses growing a stone's throw away. As I drew close to this spear-leafed plant, one of the slender buds burst open into flower before my very eyes. On film I had already seen this slow-motion opening of a bud, but this was different. It was, rather, a sudden springing into life, an instantaneous unfolding of petals. By pure chance I was there at the perfect time. I riveted all my attention on another bud which was slowly but perceptibly swelling under my fascinated gaze. This too literally popped open, followed by another and another. No less than six of these slim oval buds I saw uncoil into lovely blossoms. Their beauty was to be short-lived, though, for they would wither in the morning sun. I thought of that wistful line from Gray's "Elegy."

> Full many a flower is born to blush unseen and waste its sweetness on the desert air.

As darkness closed in on me, I heard one last sweet and clear call from a canyon wren who seemed to be bidding the dying day adieu. It was a fitting farewell.

Fifth Day

Fear knocked at the door. Faith answered. No one was there.

These solitary expeditions do not make me afraid, for I hold the firm belief that, by my being kind and caring unto the desert, the desert will in turn be kind and caring unto me. A practical person might scoff at that intangible notion, but for me it is a matter of faith. Nonetheless, when on a remote roamabout such as this, I am prey to morbid thoughts now and then. One of my mind's demons will conjure up a silly scenario in which, for example, I am savaged by a mountain lion. (Ridiculous, for such an attack has yet to be documented, to my knowledge.) Or poisoned by bad water at a spring. (A possibility but unlikely in the wilds where man doesn't have access to pollute.) In these passing moments of morbidity, I simply call on my faith in Nature and in myself — and drive off the demon who plays on susceptibility to fears primæval and irrational. He comes and goes infrequently, and each time it is faith that deals so effectively with him.

I'm of the opinion that time to oneself in the company of Nature is far more therapeutic than fear-inducing. I would even venture to say that one of the root causes for the mass neurosis of our age is the severing of the ancient bond with the Earth and its daily and perpetual rhythms. It strikes me that one of the truest paths back to healthfulness of the mind, body, and spirit is the path of closer communion with Nature and a deeper respect, appreciation, and love for her. That is a path with heart, indeed. In her wartime diary Anne Frank wrote of this:

> The best remedy for those who are afraid, lonely, or unhappy is to go outside somewhere where they can be alone with the heavens, Nature, and God. Because only then does one feel that all is as it should be and that God wishes to see people happy amidst the simple beauty of Nature. As long as this exists, and it certainly always will, I know that then there will always be comfort for every sorrow whatever the circumstances may be.

This whole day I set aside for rest and reflection though, after morning ablutions and coffee, I did take a short hike to loosen up my muscles. I even picked a pocketful of jojobas (ho-HO-bas) to add to the sackful my friend and I had gathered this past season. When hulled, they'll be sold to a seedsman who intends to sow fifteen acres of desert land with them.

Beneath a tall straight-limbed cottonwood, I sat by the green-velvet slime of a stagnant pond and watched a blue-bodied, orange-winged tarantula hawk sipping drops of water. This formidable wasp paralyzes the great birdspider with her stinger and drags it back to her burrow to lay eggs upon. Nearby was the formless, messy, but tough-stranded web of a black widow spider who had already made a meal out of various entangled insects. Above me, in the olive-green sumac bushes, phainopeplas (black crested flycatchers) wooed each other exuberantly, calling out with their one-note soft whistle. They perch high on branches and nab flies out of the air with acrobatic dives and swoops.

In mid-afternoon, deciding to head gradually homewards, I struck camp, gave thanks to Madrecita for her hospitality, and began to hike out. The heat was still fierce, so I couldn't pass up a deep, round desert pool set at the base of a sandstone terrace. The water here was chest-deep — quite unusual for the thirsting month of August. After wallowing there a while, I pressed on and finally called it a day upon reaching a stretch of level bank above the creek's floodline. Pitched the tent beside a sadly fire-gutted juniper and soon after was buffeted by a strong wind and fat drops of rain. It wasn't a cloudburst, luckily, and I managed to keep a small cooking-fire lit throughout. Being preoccupied with the thought of a stiff climb out of the canyon and the need to rise at daybreak to avoid being broiled by the sun, I had trouble in falling asleep. It must have been midnight before I did so.

Sixth Day

I rose at dawn and quickly put together my gear, not bothering with coffee or even washing. I was anxious to beat Old Sol. Setting a steady pace, I followed the narrow, winding canyon as it climbed towards its place of origin. Within the hour I could plainly see the ridge which would take me to the top of the mountain range. I had my work cut out for me, that I knew. Moments before bracing myself for the ascent, I saw movement out of the corner of my eye — there, bounding daintily up toward the skyline, ran three mule deer. Their effortless grace gave me inspiration and I was off. Not bounding, however — more like plodding. *¡Adelante y arriba!* Onward! Upward!

I took the ever-steepening slope one short step at a time and rested now and then. The gradient kept increasing until, towards the end, I was faced with a grey bluff of loose shale. For the last twenty minutes, the going was sticky. At the last stage, I was tackling the cliff on hands and knees, scrabbling my way up inch by inch and fighting the sliding rocks and gravel. One large protruding rock which had been a handhold came free from the earth and went crashing and bouncing down the slopes below me. With Horace's crook curled around a shrub — and with a prayer or two — I pulled myself up over the most treacherous part and was finally — thank God! — on firm ground. What I had dreaded all last night was now over.

I was out of the canyon, once more in familiar territory, and could enjoy the wilderness time remaining to me in peace and harmony. I made my thanksgiving and started to descend the mild incline that led to my old campsite. It was a fabulous feeling to slip out of the backpack and into the chilly, blessed waters of that shaded spring. I even took a soapbath to celebrate — away from the spring, as ever, so as not to foul it.

In the quiet of the hot afternoon, I began to think about the Great Silence that is such an intriguing and unique aspect of the Arizona desert. At times, when the wind is at rest, this silence is all-pervading, all-embracing like a divine presence. There's a wondrous stilling of all sound and it seems, inexplicably, that time itself stops. Vast sweeping landscapes, powerful vistas — and yet utterly noiseless — then, all of a sudden, a fly will come buzzing by or a bee will hum, or a breeze will sigh through the bushes. And time whirs into motion once again and the spell cast by the Eternal Silence is gently broken. Sometimes, beyond the silence, I seem to hear a distant drone but though I'm convinced it has no man-made origin, I'm unable to pin-point its source. My name for this mystery is "a cosmic murmur," and I leave it at that.

Shadows were lengthening when I had six visitors in the campsite. I was writing this journal with my back propped up against a log. A series of low grunts made me look up. A little herd of javelina wended its way up to the bank from the spring below and disappeared into the bush, grunting contentedly. A minute later, a husky male, acting, I suppose, as the rear-guard, peeled off the trail, stood in the sunlit clearing some twenty yards from me, sniffed the air suspiciously, and looked me up and down a few times. Satisfied that I meant no harm to his herd, he calmly wandered off and picked up the trail again. To see these javelina — and to have been at peace with them — somehow put a seal of Nature's acceptance on the wilderness experience that was drawing to a close for me. Even a noisy band of bluejays seemed to chatter their approval.

Seventh Day

This was my final morning in the desert wilds. Leaving behind some dry crumbled tortillas for the resident skunk, I set off homewards with gladness in my heart for all that *Madrecita* had so generously revealed to me in my days of aloneness.

Conclusion

As the years pass and I become closer to the desert, I tend to quietly regard myself as a sort of latter-day Apache. I roam the desert and feel at one with it. I'm always stepping from rock to rock so as not to leave tracks. I drink belly-down at creeks and springs. I nibble on wild edibles and eat camp food with fierce gusto. I strive to treat wild animals, plants, and insects with the utmost respect. I make sudden political raids on despoiler-developers from time to time and then melt back into the hills. And I conserve wood by building tiny campfires. Like the Apaches, I believe that man should view himself as the caretaker, steward, or custodian of the land, not the owner of it. And I know for myself that there is more true knowledge to be acquired and more wisdom to be gained from the open book of Nature than from all the books in all the libraries of the whiteman's world.

Therefore, it is fitting that I should end this account with what I consider to be a most moving Indian prayer:

O Great Spirit, whose voice I hear in the wind and who gives life to all my people, hear me — for I am a young man small and weak. I seek your strength and wisdom so I may teach my people. I seek strength, Father, not to be better than my brother but to be able to fight my greatest enemy, myself. I seek your wisdom, the secrets you have hidden under every leaf and stone. May my hands respect the many things you have done and may my ears be ever sharp to hear your voice. May I always walk in your Beauty and my eyes ever behold the red and purple sunsets so that, when life fades like the setting sun, my spirit will come to you without shame.

V: Al Yermo Otra Vez: To the Wilds Once Again

Monday June 13th to Sunday June 19th 1983

First Day

> I love all waste
> And solitary places; where we taste
> The pleasure of believing what we see
> Is boundless, as we wish our souls to be.
>
> — Percy Bysshe Shelley

From on high, perched and peering, the pale-breasted hawk screamed a welcome — or was it a warning? The last sight of civilization was a cloud of dust as my friend drove off, honking her horn at the wayward calf prancing in front of her on the rough road. I was off again on a solo trek into the wilderness, for my annual spell of solitary refinement.

The time was 5:30 p.m. and although the searing summer sun was still high in the sky I was later in setting off than I would have liked. So I struck a steady pace along a cattle track and the grazing range-cows watched me warily with that bovine curiosity of theirs. Among the milling herd was a zebu, a grey bull of African origin with a humped back, enormous ears, and a pair of wicked curved horns. The cattle bellowed mournfully as I trudged past. An hour of meandering downwards on a track that had seen no wheels for a long time brought me to a point where cross-country trekking was required — or so I surmised.

Down an endless slope populated with aromatic junipers and cruel cat-claw bushes, I hiked, slipping on the loose decomposed granite from time to time and cursing the snatching, scratching chaparral. My destination, the canyon floor where water flowed, didn't seem to get any closer. The backpack, a deadweight with its cargo of food and camping equipment, strained at my aching shoulders. The evening breeze died and the sultry stillness of the heavy air added to my discomfort. But of course I pressed on, with a watchful eye on the failing light and a longing look at the winding ribbon of greenery at the base of the *bajada* I was wearily descending.

In spite of the physical fatigue, my spirits were high and my heart was singing with the joyousness that always accompanies my extended periods of aloneness in this lovely, lonely land of little rain. Solitude is meat and drink to me. Nothing can match the spirited sensation of abandoning, if only for a week, all one's responsibilities and obligations to the harrowed human race. Walt Whitman put it so well in his "Open Road":

> Afoot & light-hearted I take to the open road,
> Healthy, free, the world before me, the long brown path leading
> wherever I choose.
> Henceforth I ask not good fortune, I myself am good fortune.
> Henceforth I whimper no more, postpone no more,
> need nothing.
> Done with indoor complaints, libraries, querulous criticisms,
> strong and content, I travel the open road.
> The earth — this is sufficient.

So few seek pure solitude in the broad bosom of Madrecita — and so many should for their own peace of mind:

> Give me solitude,
> Give me Nature,
> Give me O Nature
> Your primal sanities!

Whitman again. He knew, didn't he?

I continued slithering and sliding downwards until, at last, I came to a narrow dry wash strewn with the most colorful mix of bright white and burnt-orange rocks. However, my poetic appreciation for the many hues of Nature's palette was at its lowest ebb and all I could think about was cool, clear water.

Soon I smelled it in the air, which cooled noticeably many yards before reaching the blessed creek in the main canyon. Glory be! I had made it down those interminable inclines in two hours flat. There remained enough daylight for me to find a soft and sandy spot for camping. As I slaked my thirst, belly-down at the creek, I glanced up and saw two javelina doing likewise. They were fifty yards away and, though short-sighted, they sniffed me out and dashed off into the undergrowth, snuffling and snorting — with a tiny petrified, panting piglet bringing up the rear.

What a wonderful wildlife sighting and so soon. A good omen, I thought. Moments later I had torn off my sweaty, gritty T shirt and shorts and splashed, naked as a nymph, into a chest-high pool formed at the base of a streamside sycamore. "Oooh!" I said rapturously as I sank beneath the still surface of this cold and crystal pool. It felt fabulous. Had darkness not been closing in on me, I would've wallowed there forever. The last golden gleams from the sunken sun caught the skin of my naked body and it shone coppery as though I were Indian, a fleeting moment of a sort of aboriginal magic.

In the dark, over a small pit-fire, I cooked a pan of rice and brewed what the Mexicans call *café arriero*, muleskinner's coffee. I was washed and fed — and sublimely happy. Stretched out on my sleeping bag, listening to the cry of the poorwill and the rustling of some rodent in the rushes, looking up at the luminous heavens, I said this prayer of thanks: "You give me so much, Madrecita, you give me so much."

Second Day

> Nature is like a silent but sympathetic companion in whose company we retain solitude, with whom we can walk, and talk or be silent.
>
> — Henry David Thoreau

I woke up several hours before first light and, dazzled by the stars and excited by the new adventure, never went back to sleep. It was a perfect night with a light caressing breeze. For my sleeplessness I was rewarded with the glimpse of a meteor streaking across the southern sky. It lasted but one splendid instant and then vanished into eternity.

Birdsong began at daybreak with the plaintive call of the poorwill. I heeded his first call and got up. Shortly after 6 a.m., my belly awash with Mexican coffee, I set off — traveling light — to the upper part of the creek. I was surprised to see it swiftly dry up, leaving encrusted sun-bleached algae on its bed-rocks. As desert streams do, it surfaced again near the foot of a jagged, ragged ridge of quartz. This impressive formation, rampart-like, was as much as twenty feet high in places. When the water picked up again, the big trees — willow, sycamore, and cottonwood, so much a part of the riparian habitat in Arizona — appeared.

While exploring a cave, approached by way of a steep cat-claw covered hill — with much slipping and cursing — I came across Indian (wild) tobacco. I harvested a handful of the furry, sticky leaves for my new friend, Berniece Falling Leaves, and set them out to sun-dry in a rock hollow. Descending gingerly, I got a passing look at the graceful back of a black hawk which flew directly below me. And then I watched, with envy, as a whitewing dove, cooing soulfully, glided effortlessly from a pinnacle of quartz rock across the wide expanse of the canyon to the top of a giant saguaro. Isn't there an old song that goes, "Oh, for the wings of dove"? How fine to fly free — on no other fuel but seeds.

I kept rock-hopping my way upstream and fell once but not badly. Each time I recover safely from a sudden slip, I give thanks — for I know only too well what problems a broken limb could cause me — and others. By the grace of God, in a thousand and one hikes that has never happened. Strong hiker though I am, I'm not so foolish as to assume that it never will.

During this wandering along by the twisting, shaded creek, I beheld a marvellous thing. A fawn, all on its own, stepped daintily down to the water's edge to drink. Unobserved by this delicate creature (which, fawn in colour, suited its name), I settled down on a rock and kept still. It was perhaps fifty yards away and seemed perpetually poised to flee — for it would look up with great ears pricked and sense out possible danger. Only after minutes, when I stood up, did it bound away up the bank. Once the sun bathed its hide in light — and there was a radiance to the animal. It is said that in remote sections of Alaska wild animals, being unaccustomed to man's presence, have no fear of him. Not so in Arizona, where they are hounded and hunted by marauding man.

Nearly three hours after leaving base camp, I came upon the desolate sight of a huge and living cottonwood tree that had fallen across the creek in a a tight spot and smashed itself against a solid rock face. Unhappily, its massive weight had crushed a smaller sycamore tree on the other side. There were broken limbs scattered in the creek. The cottonwood's corpse had created a solid natural bridge across the water.

Wanting to be back at base camp by high noon (for eating and writing, in that order), I turned around at a place where springwater gushed out of a cliff into the main stream, pure and sweet. A heartening sight in this land of searing summers. I'd scarcely gone ten yards when with an exclamation of "Whoops!" I came to a definite halt.

There, a few feet from where I'd stopped, stretched out and with its scaly, lipless mouth touching the water was an Arizona black rattlesnake. It stayed motionless, ignoring my blundering presence so completely that I feared it might have drowned. In order to find out, I climbed up behind the protection of a rock and, with every gentleness, reached down with Horace, my Yorkshire shepherd's crook, and touched the snake on its tail. It was alive, all right. It gave the faintest of rattles, withdrew its charcoal-grey head from the creek, and stared at me with eyes reptilian and glittering. But it did not coil, nor did it rattle. It was emotionally well-adjusted, I'd say. I thanked it for putting up with me so graciously, made my farewell, and continued on my way.

I cannot abide the wanton killing of snakes, venomous or otherwise. My own experiences with rattlesnakes have been numerous. In no way are they the vicious creatures they are made out to be. On the contrary, they are, for the most part, even-tempered, gentlemanly in their warning signals, and liable to bite only under extreme provocation. The human being, *Homo rapiens*, is a much nastier piece of work. For those with the all-too-common phobia of snakes, I strongly recommend that they read D. H. Lawrence's poem, "Snake." He refers to the snake met at a waterhole as "one of the Lords of life" and I heartily agree with him.

I retraced my steps to the camping spot. Having wolfed down a lunch of tortillas and sardines washed down with piping hot tea, I packed up all the gear and, true to the form of "mad dogs and Englishmen," staggered back with my burden — under the midday sun — to the heavily shaded area near the quartz-ridge pool. There to pitch camp and stay put for several days. After that, I would have eaten down the ponderous weight of that bloody backpack. I once saw a Tarahumara Indian (in Chihuahua, Mexico) gaze amazed upon my cumbersome backpack — as he ran light-footedly and baggage-free up a Sierra Madre goat path. Truly, the bulging backpack is the whiteman's burden.

At one o'clock I settled back against the stout trunk of an old willow and began the discipline of a diary. Last year on my solo trek I treated myself to no writing — but, alas, my Puritan work ethic won't allow me to get away with it this year. So there I sat after four hours, numb in bum and bleary-eyed, still writing away. I liked the story told about the Prince of Wales who, when presented personally with the many volumes of *The Decline & Fall of the Roman Empire* by its distinguished author, merely said, "Scribble, scribble, scribble, eh, Mr Gibbon?"

It seemed that on this trip I didn't even have to bestir myself to see wildlife. Propped up against the tree trunk, I heard a rustle in the dead twigs beside me. There, sinuous and splendid, was an alternately-marked black and white kingsnake. He appeared to be seeking a meal for he eased his head and the front portion of his body into a hole that could've housed a rodent. But it obviously didn't because, after a cursory check, he pulled himself out and meandered off to mousier parts. A friend once brought a similar snake up to my cabin and released it in the woodpile — but I've not seen it since.

A gorgeous butterfly landed close to my scribbling spot. I'd never before seen such magnificent markings. Its wings were velvet black, tipped with round splotches of orange; across them diagonally ran closely-joined circles of white. I thought of dear Edie H. the butterfly lady and reminded myself to tell her of this lightsome encounter.

Quiet as a churchmouse while filling these pages, I'd been hearing grunts and snorts coming from the brush on the hillside just above a cattail marsh. Had to be a herd of javelina but, even with a sneaky barefoot stroll, I'd be damned if I could spot them. The Abominable Pigmen, maybe? If so, they could join me at the trough for dinner. (Those first pages had taken me five hours and countless gnat bites to finish — but no matter, it was a literary labour of love.)

Evidently I'd chosen a special spot to camp. It was the site of a natural phenomenon, a prickly pear cactus growing high off the ground in the crotch of a cottonwood tree. I once saw a prickly pear sprouting forth from a saguaro, but that was a long time ago.

Supper consisted of brown rice and "generic" chicken sausages which look like hell but are fairly flavorful. I experimented with saccharin in my coffee — but when I tossed in four tablets they foamed up like Alka-Seltzer, which was rather alarming. Not a bad sweetener, though, and so much lighter to carry than sugar.

Those tiny, invisible biting insects of the evening — no-see-ums — were doing to me what they were created to do. I realized that my nearness to the swampy spot would also mean mosquitoes. So up went the screened tent which had not been needed the night before. This enabled me to light candles and read a while before nodding off to sleep. The book, appropriately, was *Mosquito Coast*, by Paul Theroux. After the day's exertions and that vigorous hiking in the heat, sleep came swiftly.

Third Day

> He who is in harmony with Nature hits the mark without effort, and apprehends the truth without thinking.
>
> — Confucius

About thirty minutes away from where I'd camped, there was a many-ledged cliff face set back from the watercourse. On one of those ledges, near the brink of the cliff and yet not accessible from it, was a broad nest of sticks and twigs. It belonged to a red-tailed hawk who was highly indignant at my passing by. There was much circling and crying and complaining from that beautiful bird but, intending it no harm, I was of mind to ignore its carryings-on.

Below this nest on a smooth face of whitish rock were some vivid Indian pictographs. These rock paintings, unique in my experience, seemed to portray a giant centipede and several suns. Their colour was of the brightest red. Had they used some sort of red clay such as ochre, perhaps? The only reason they had held their strong colour and clarity of form was that they were sheltered from the elements by a rock overhang. Yesterday I had squinted at them in the noon sunlight, I found myself wondering whether the spirits of those prehistoric artists still roamed these great and secret places.

The canopy of tree foliage under which I reposed was a haven for many birds — and how gaily they greeted the break of day. My own joy was not as manifest this morning since I slept in till six. A banana, an orange, and coffee took care of my breakfast. By seven a.m. I was off on my explorations, light of heart and full of anticipation. The sun had already cleared the canyon walls. As usual, I saluted his smiling face with a "*¡Buenos dias, Sol!*"

Suddenly a dark shadow moved quickly over the surface of the glistening creek. I glanced upwards at a zone-tailed hawk, silently swooping through the canyon treetops. I knew that there was a pair nesting in the area because yesterday they had caused a commotion when I went by. It was an odd noise they made while wheeling above me, a cross between a shriek and a wheeze — a shreeze, could I say?

Today I swung up a side canyon through which water was flowing. To hike the upper desert, heat-stricken and waterless, was to invite unnecessary risks, and I loved life too dearly for that. As I danced my way up this tight arroyo, springing from rock to rock, I became aware of how we learn the art of physical balance in the wilderness. No balance is demanded of us in day-to-day life, for everywhere we go the way has been evened out for us with asphalt or concrete. But here in the outback (as the Aussies call it), nothing is truly flat and every step is an act of balancing that becomes instinctive with experience. Nature also teaches us what we do not learn in civilization: how to observe and be sharply aware of what goes on around us. That is perhaps why I usually spot people I know before they spot me. In Aldous Huxley's imaginary island (called Pala), the enlightened inhabitants trained mynah birds to fly free and to cry, "Pay attention! Pay attention!" Some of them called out, "Be here now, boys!" I thought of that as I wandered along and caught myself mentally ahead in the future. It was a never-ending discipline to live fully and vividly in the present. And so, for the umpteenth time, I gently rebuked myself for that future-tripping and said aloud, half in jest, half in seriousness, "If you're not being here now, you might not be there then."

After shouldering a way through dense streamside vegetation, I came upon a sacred datura showing off a single, superb moonflower; trumpetlike in shape and snowy-white, this magnificent specimen was a full four inches in diameter. It gave off a musky aroma, sweet and sensuous, and I buried my mouth and nose full into its generous openness. If eaten, the seeds, the flowers, the leaves, the roots of this mysterious plant are said to drive men mad. The shamans of yore knew well its secrets.

An hour's hiking brought a sound of cascading water to my ears. Rounding a brushy bend, I found a waterfall, some thirty feet high and of extraordinary beauty. Where the sun-sparkling stream poured over its lip, a sycamore's exposed roots clutched the wet cliff-face like great gnarled fingers. From them sprouted leafy seedlings. The water, falling in four distinct rivulets over a mat of green and golden algae, was fine-framed by a hanging garden of pale yellow columbines. An enchanted place — for, as I marvelled at it, a hummingbird alighted three feet from me on the spongy carpet of algae and sipped water with his needle-pointed beak. That was a magical first for me. Though this hidden cascade was the climax of the morning's ramblings, something urged me to press on a little farther, even though it entailed climbing high and dry to get around the impasse made by the waterfall.

I scrabbled my way up the burning red earth slope and was moving back down to the creek level when a huge bird flew up and away from below. I saw its massive brown-feathered hulk and royal raptor's head from my position above. I believed it to be a golden eagle. Its prodigious wingspan and slow, deliberate flapping motion resembled no hawk I'd ever seen. It kept a low flight. I watched it a full minute and then hurried down to the hummock on which it had been perched. Just two clues remained of this regal bird — chalk-white droppings and a small, mottled light-brown feather. The latter I stowed safely away with the collection of bluejay feathers, found earlier at the scene of perhaps a hawk's feast. How remarkable to have had an intimate encounter with both the tiniest and greatest of birds, all within a matter of minutes.

As it happened, my electrifying moments were not over for the day. Having picked my wending way back down this side-creek, I was within sight of the big trees in the main canyon when a familiar heart-stopping buzz sent me leaping to the left. Yes, it was my old friend Crotalus again, advising me in startling but courteous fashion to stay clear, which of course I did. This was a colourful yellow-chequered black-tailed rattlesnake, close to four feet long. Considerately, he stopped rattling right away and, sensing no malice, lost interest in me. Seems that I was the only one still rattled. I stood quietly, fascinated to know what he was about. It turned out that he really wanted to cross that creek. What he did, in fact, was rather interesting. He sought a way across from rock to rock and didn't apparently want his underbelly wet, though it did touch the water now and then. I've studied snakes in the wild before. Their method of locomotion is not only a minor miracle but it also happens to be somewhat erotic — for those of us with fertile, feverish, and phallic imaginations. They have an undulating, controlled writhing which, translated into human terms, is uninhibitedly sensual. It is said that certain lascivious ladies in ancient Rome put snakes to a curious use, and I can see why.

While maneuvering across the creek, this particular fellow used his body as a bridge between rocks. He was able to draw the length of it across empty spaces — in rigid fashion and without dragging limply behind him. When his head was still, the rear part of his body continued to inch lithely forward — and throughout this snake-symphony of motion, his rattle stayed upright. Wet rattles make miserable music, no doubt. After he'd made the grand crossing and was peering perplexedly at the raised bank, I waved goodbye and thanked him for the peaceful encounter.

I was back well before high noon and so slipped down to the emerald pool at the bottom of the quartz water chute — and in my nymph-like nudity was nibbled on shamelessly by darting fishes and titillating tadpoles.

As I write here in mid-afternoon beneath a roughed-barked ash, I see the vine entwining it is hung with clusters of plump green grapes. They'll not be ripe while I'm in residence, alas. There's light, wispy cloud flecking the sky today, but it holds no promise of rain to sweeten the fiery breath of summer.

I've been having dinner later than usual. Perhaps the heat is putting a curb on my appetite. The fire-pit in scooped-out sand serves my cooking needs well. When I leave, there won't remain a trace of it. The acrid smell of woodsmoke is primitive and pleasurable though, when the wind changes, it can set the eyes a-streaming. Nothing's more effective in driving off midges and mosquitoes. After more rice and chicken sausages — variety of menu is not my forte on wilderness trips — I waited till nightfall and crawled into my low-slung tent. My night-reading lasted only as long as the candle stubs. Sleep claimed me fast.

Fourth Day

> I passionately love the beauties of Nature; the marvels of the hand of God transport me with such admiration that, in comparison, the finest work of man seems only trivial.
> — Abbé Armand David

The broad side-canyon I chose to explore this morning was dry to begin with -- but then that desert miracle happened and, unexpectedly, there was first the sound and then the sight of trickling water. To this desert wayfarer, a two-litre plastic throwaway filled with water is all that stands between vibrant life and a disagreeable death. So when water is chanced upon in the wilds, it is indeed a benediction. Only fools in cities play with water. Only those hostile to our precious desert build fountains in hills and ludicrous lakes where once the creosote grew. For these desert dilettantes and despoilers, I have a short prayer (or is it a curse?): "O Great Sun in heaven, dry 'em up and drive 'em out!"

I have bellied-down to a hundred desert streams and drunk deeply and gratefully from them — and never once have I taken sick from doing so. Which means that I've yet to find a decomposing cow around the bend and upstream from me. And since, in everyday life, I am a drinker of water and not of beer these days, I must take exception to the drinking man who said he never drank water because, in his words, "It goes under bridges and fish fornicate in it." Water is life — and I love them both.

In this canyon I was newly discovering, the trickle of water became a flowing stream; because of it, the tall trees came into leafy, lofty being. When the stream made an oxbow bend, I found myself ambling through a cathedral of towering trees which thinned out into a mesquite *bosque*. It was staggering to think of the mighty thirst that this gallery of trees would have in the height of the summer. It's estimated that a cottonwood, for example, can suck up 200 gallons per day; however, at the end of the day, it will release that which it does not use.

I might add that the average resident of Phoenix, a much smaller life-form than the stately cottonwood, uses 266 gallons a day. What he releases (by necessity rather than choice) takes five more gallons of fresh water to dispose of it. Criminal.

As I forged on up the canyon, I picked up a cattle trail which had been "maintained" by Mexican vaqueros. There was much uncalled-for slashing and slicing of juniper branches and, in two places, old picnic trash that included a salsa can and tortilla wrappers. Since all these canyons had been spared the blight of human garbage, I was particularly angered by this cowboy littering. So I gathered it up into an empty plastic bucket and left the following note:

VAQUEROS. MUY PUERCA LA BASURA. A LLEVARLA FUERA DE ACÁ. (Cowboys. Litter is very filthy. Take it out of here.)

The second lot of trash produced stronger language in my note:

CABRONES PUERCOS — which means *dirty cuckolds* in English. (*Cabron* is fighting talk in Mexico. It signifies that the man wears horns because his woman is being bedded by another man — but, of course, it is used loosely and rarely in the literal sense.)

Obviously I was upset.

I must mention that I have as much love for the Mexican people as I have for my own. They have shown me tremendous kindness on my many trips south of the border. One of the sad realities of Mexico, however, is a couldn't-care-less attitude to the ubiquitous litter there.

Though the summer sun had taken a fierce hold on this land and springtime was but a cool memory, the desert was not without flowers. At this time, the widespread prickly pear (which invades overgrazed areas) was displaying both pink and yellow rose-like blossoms soon to be purple pulpy fruits. Along the creek, benefiting from the damp rich earth, lived Indian paintbrushes, red and radiant. And on drier ground, in the desert itself, grew the mauve mats of trailing windmills. Here and there stood a slender swaying prickly poppy, nicknamed the cowboy's fried egg for its round, flat white flower with a yellow yolk-like centre. I saw one pretty patch of off-white morning glories, as delicate as fairycups.

The sun beat brazenly down as I followed the cow trail out of the cool of the canyon up on to steep and open ground. A trail leading to I know not where is like a Pied Piper to me. I simply cannot leave it be and turn back. And so, heating up along with the swift-climbing sun and moving away from a sure water source, I sweated up this stony path until it levelled out on a saddle bright with dried grass the color of flax. The trail then dropped down to what appeared to be an oasis of greenery in the fold of a red-cinder mountain.

I said to myself sternly, "To the spring — and no further!," and continued on down. I was not welcome, however. A nesting Cooper's hawk, with eyesight for which it is famous in our language, spotted me straightaway and began cackling like a persecuted parrot. From ground level I could make out a large nest of branches and sticks, built fairly low in the thick limbs of a spreading willow. Keeping a sharp eye out for the irate hawk, I filled a waterjug from a clear pool at the foot of a mossy rock-slide. Then I noticed that the trail did not end there but that it ascended the opposite slope. "Aha," thought I, "if I climb up it a ways, I can perhaps look down into the nest." So I scrambled and was treated to a sight that made me chuckle with delight. There, just below me and in full view, was a comical quintet: five chicks, all bluff and fluff, each as big as two clenched fists, not moving a feather, and sitting upright and staring at me so solemnly.

God, what I would've given for a good camera. It was a picture of absolute preciousness and the memory of it will forever bring a smile to my lips and a tear to my eye. Mother hawk, however, didn't give a damn about my poetic sentiments for her blessed brood. She wanted me out of the neighbourhood and fast. All I saw was this brown-feathered bullet speeding straight at me. I waved Horace wildly. At the last moment she veered off into the trees with an exasperated cry. Feeling that she'd had grief enough with just my presence (however harmless), I quickly left her territory.

This farthest point of my hike was the highest in excitement. And I knew then what it was that had impelled me, against my better judgment, to leave the shaded canyon behind and push on up that dry and dusty track. "Faint heart never won fair chick." The downward climb to base camp was anti-climactic, sticky and tiring. It took all of two hours and a quarter. But in spite of fatigue, I still managed to step around spiders' webs instead of crashing through them. (That, by the way, is the height of consideration on any hike, anywhere.)

The most eventful thing on the return trip was brushing up against the dried seed pods of some locoweed and jumping a foot in the air at the startling rattle. I did notice a prolific stand of sycamore seedlings in the creek bed and realized that this tree has to produce many for the few to survive. Most of these, for instance, will be scoured out by the next flashflood during the summer rains. And cattle cause them untold damage.

Upon getting back to camp, I made a beeline for the pool and plunged in. "Glorious!" was all I could say, "Glorious!"

This afternoon, cleansed by the creek, well-fed and rested, I leaned back against my special tree trunk and started scribbling away at this journal again. I seemed to be in the spirit of writing — but it was, as always, a consuming affair.

A little after one o'clock I was quite surprised to hear a poorwill calling. It must've got day and night mixed up, because it's supposed to be a nocturnal bird which feeds on insects. In fact, it gave its call several times during the afternoon. How strange.

I saw a high-speed chase between black tree lizards which ended in one of them hurling itself off a vertical branch into mid-air. Could that have been some bizarre courtship ritual indicating that lovin' lizards like leapin'? Around here the brittle fallen leaves always seem to be a-rustle with skittering lizards — and there's never a shortage of boastful males doing their reptilian push-ups, inflating their dewlaps, or showing off their brilliant blue bellies. (Worth a try sometime.)

Wonderful to relate, a dainty blue damsel-fly set herself down on the end of my ballpen as I was poised to write. Any symbolism in that? Was it a message from Madrecita?

In the early evening, when the light was failing and the no-see-ums were driving me up the canyon wall, I sauntered down to the pool for a final dip of the day. A movement in the desert broom on the edge of the eroded streambank attracted my eye. It was a skunk shuffling around over there. Wanting to be neighborly, I called out, "Howdy, Skunk!" It took a dim view of my good ol' boy friendliness and bolted off into the bushes. What incredible luck I was having with wildlife spotting on this adventure. Dusk was giving away to moon-shadows when I came back to camp to find that the nearby datura moonflower (on which I'd been keeping a close eye) had fully opened in the short fifteen minutes I'd been gone. "You opened without me, damn it!" I said peevishly to this floral masterpiece whose heady perfume was already filling the evening air and luring insects into her silky depths. Nearby was another datura bloom, ready to unfurl, so I touched it softly and blew gently on it. The petals parted a little and I could even see the anthers inside — but this Sacred One was not about to put on the main show for my benefit. Obviously Mother Nature had not been fooled by this foreplay. So I gave up on my teasing games and, a little disgruntled, unzipped my fly-screen and turned in for the night.

Croaks and cavortings came from the marsh later on. I thought of an old English song from childhood:

> Froggie would a-wooing go...
> Hey, ho! said Rollie!

Fifth Day

> The natural world is a spiritual house.
>
> — Baudelaire

As I pulled on my pair of odd boots, I noticed a hole in the sole of the right one — and fervently hoped that it would hold up for the remainder of the trek. Ever since I discovered a dead and dried scorpion hanging from my sock near the big toe, I've made a point of shaking out boots before putting them on. Why odd boots? Well, out of two old and battered pairs, I had a good left one and a reasonable right one. Since one is a brown suede and the other a black high-ankle army boot, they look odd, but, what the hell? They wear well. I told a friend, who was quite amused by this, that they'll do a fair job of keeping away the evil spirits.

The canyon I chose to penetrate this morning had a narrow mouth which was dry. I was, of course, carrying the two-litre plastic bottle but it was leaking through the cap — an annoyance since I had to hold it upright in my hand. Change of circumstance can certainly alter attitude, if only temporarily. This type of plastic throwaway which normally I detest had become of critical importance to me. Without its capacity to contain water, I was to all intents and purposes chained to the creekside. This unethical, crass, non-returnable creation of the beverage industry had become a godsend in the wilderness — and to me, the arch-enemy of the throwaway. Ironic, eh?

I got off to a fine start by stumbling across a broken metate lying amongst the jumble of flood-smoothed rocks in the bone-dry creekbed. Metates are hand-hollowed rocks used by the earlier peoples of the Southwest to grind corn and seeds. I hid this one so that it would never be removed from the place to which it prehistorically belonged. I passed by a datura plant, set in the sandy soil that it loved. It was bearing a dozen beauteous blooms and I knew that, being born of the night, they would wilt and wither before the sun had reached its zenith. The poet Keats wrote, "A thing of beauty is a joy forever," but the life of a flower is fleeting and only in the memory can it remain a joy forever.

This chasm I was venturing up was distinctly female in nature. The parched dryness had been left behind. This twisting and tight gorge was now damp and luxuriant with ferns and flowers. There were rock-clefts padded with dark moss, secret fissures criss-crossed with silver-shining spider webs, moist mysterious caverns laced with dripping fronds, grottoes beneath rounded boulder mounds hung with gossamer threads, and, where the ravine boxed up, a single ribbon of water falling twenty feet into what could have been a jungle pool. Framing the silver ribbon on both sides were long dank strands of light-green algae from which rhythmically fell bright beads of water. I found myself standing spellbound in this place. There was a languorous, almost seductive air about it and it played powerfully on my senses. It had a primordial Garden of Eden feeling to it and, as I looked around, wonderingly, I could see an abundance of wild edibles — grapes, lemonade berries, sumac fruits, hackberries, choke-cherries, cattails, prickly pear, and even the promise of honey — for up against the cliff, in a brown-stained hollow, was a thriving bee hive. This was surely a dell where elves frolicked and if that that moment I had heard the pipes of Pan drifting through the canyon, I would not have been amazed.

I lingered there like a lotus-eater, dreamily — and then to break the spell and regain my familiar desert, I scaled the canyonside and emerged once more into the hammering sun-light. How different that experience had been from the other canyons which were so masculine in their aspect. They had seemed open and extrovert, rough and tough in texture, defiant, arrogant in their strength, bold and brazen.

I came back down by way of an obscure cowpath that meandered along the spine of a long hog's back (the western name for a ridge). It was gratifying to note that four days of hard-core hiking had removed the better part of my bean belly, and, as usual, I regretted not having weighed myself before leaving. It has never ceased to astonish me that people will pay good money to take off weight in soulless spas when they could do it for nothing in the outdoors and have some serenity thrown in too. But then I'm hopelessly biased.

Nietsche said that he always trusted those thoughts he had while walking. I agree with him, by and large, but some of mine are rather strange. Today, for example, it occurred to me that, when this trek is over, I will have gone a week without seeing my own face — because I didn't bring a mirror. Such a revelation is of no use to me whatsoever but think about it: How many people can say that they've spent a full seven days without once gawking at their own faces?

On the descent back to my outpost, I frightened a cicada which in turn frightened me by flying out of a bush and narrowly missing my face. They're curious insects, those chubby cicadas and appear to enjoy the most arid spots and the hottest temperatures. At murderous midday, when all other creatures (except *Homo sapiens*) are doing the sensible thing and lying low, the cicada is shrilling away in some burning bush with a sound like a tinny telephone ring. I must admit that I too love the all-embracing womb-warmth of the summer sun — but the silly cicada overdoes it a bit.

If home is where the heart is, then this canyon must be home — for herein doth lie my heart. To round the sweeping bend in the main creek and see my tent in the distant trees beckoning me like a blue beacon — that indeed was a homecoming. Such a noble and sincerely-felt sentiment was soon dimmed by the common-place reality of having to pluck fox-tails from my socks above boot-line. But this time, beside myself with impatience, I took drastic measures and, wildly wielding my French country knife, cut the infested ankle-parts from the main socks and tossed them in the campfire. I all of a sudden became the owner of a jagged pair of Peds.

This evening I'd finished supper and, in the last light of day, was pottering around the camp when I heard a god-awful growl from upstream. It made my blood run cold. *Mountain lion* was my first thought. Whatever it was, I wanted to see it badly — so, barefoot, raced along the boulder-strewn bank of the creek, stopping now and then to listen for more sounds. With considerable stealth (and in this I was helped by bare feet, quite noiseless), I approached close to where I thought the beast might be. I felt like an Apache stalking his prey. Standing stock still, my eyes roved the thick stand of arrow-weed on the opposite bank.

Dark grey shapes were moving through the brush and then I heard grufflings and gruntings and snortings — a whole herd of javelina, those pig-like peccaries. Even after they had broken out of the bushes that concealed them and come down to the creek itself, they didn't get wind of me for a while. I was in full view of them — but still as a statue. There must've been twenty of them milling around the bluish-grey rocks — and I noticed a baby staying close to its mother, squealing. There seemed to be a lone male sentinel watching out for them. He stood guard on a rise above the creek and though this husky brute appeared to be looking my way, he gave no warning. It was actually another adult that picked up my fragrant scent and how that snout was a-sniffing in my direction. When he sounded the alarm — *Hoof it, y'all!* — only five peeled off from the main herd and galloped away. The others had a delayed reaction and it took them ten or more seconds to follow suit. Some shot up a dry wash, others took to the slope — all of them had their black bristles standing straight up on their backs. The baby went prancing off, following up the rear at a fair clip — as tiny as he was, he was no pig in a poke.

After all that excitement (much better than the six o'clock news), I lay back in the sand and let darkness close in on me. The moon was already casting her luminous light on the sun-weary desert and the evening star shone supremely in the west. The crickets started up their nightly performance and the bats came darting out of their cliff crevices and fluttered freely above me in their ceaseless search for supper. I gazed at the moon's gleaming crescent, I looked at the emerging pin points of stars, I glanced at the free-wheeling bats and tuned in to the crickets' chorus. All's well and in order with the cosmos and the Earth, I thought. Why then is Man out of step with all this? Since he is not in harmony with the cosmos and the natural world, could it be that he really does not belong here?

One thing I know — and he knows — Nature can get along very well indeed without him. Nature has no need of him whatsoever. Perhaps it is this knowledge, so shattering to his swollen ego, that makes him lash out at the wondrous works of Nature with a destructiveness that is truly appalling. I believe I now understand why Alan Watts wrote

> Increasingly, the world around us looks as if we hated it.

Sixth Day

I stepped on my disposable plastic razor this morning — and broke it. I'm glad I broke it but I'm ashamed that I bought the wretched thing in the first place. Karma, I suppose. I don't use the disposables usually and I've even given up aerosol shaving cream for an old-fashioned brush and soap scraps. When I packed it, I was just thinking of cutting down on weight. Why shave out here, anyway? There's just me and God, thank God. Well, it seems to be an idiosyncracy of the English, one of the few I haven't managed to discard in the past twenty-one years. If they're not cleanshaven, wherever they might be, they think they're letting the side down. What side? The only side around here is a canyonside. Ah, well, a misplaced boot scrunched that philosophical problem for me. Reflecting on another desert, another Englishman in another time, I remember the movie

Lawrence of Arabia, and Lowell Thomas, the reporter, asking, "Colonel Lawrence, why do you love the desert?"

"Because it's clean," was the answer.

I doubt that he was talking about litter, either. We certainly couldn't say the same where that's concerned, could we? Though we might be able to one day — if we ever get a blessed bottle-return bill passed in the state legislature.

Being the day before I was to leave this desert place (already?), the morning's side hike was the last one. I set forth a few minutes before six. When I felt the searing force of the sun, I was happy for an early start. I kept to the creek bed, which went dry on me fairly soon. The giant saguaros on the slopes joining this broad stretch of the canyon were setting green fruit which would ripen by month's end. Some still had waxy-white blossoms crowning their tips. How on earth did they stand this punishing heat day after rainless day, I wondered? They even grew thickest and sturdiest on south-facing slopes — where the sun strikes longest. Let a man or woman stand out there, without water or shade, for just one summer's day — and he or she'd be toppled over dead and dehydrated by evening. For their tenacity and extraordinary survival skills, let alone their botanical uniqueness, these saguaros and all other plants of our great Sonoran desert should be consecrated. But what do we do instead — in our infinite wisdom? We desecrate them and denature this marvellous desert they live in — with golf courses and other grotesque greenery.

Pressing on down the wide swath of the canyon and hoping for a renewal of the water flow, I was suddenly (it happens that way!) summoned by the call of nature. This is a delicate matter to broach but since there's a tale to be told of Yankee ingenuity in this case, I shall tell it. Bluntly, I was without toilet paper and with no running water in the immediate vicinity, I was unable to use the moisture method that has been successfully employed in India since time immemorial. I was in a fundamental fix. Nature was calling me urgently. What to do? In the nick of time, I remembered Persian friends telling me long ago of the wiping way of their desert nomads — Seven Smooth Stones. As wild and barbaric as it sounded to a man from the four-ply, fully-absorbent toilet culture, I had no alternative but to try it. With the utmost care and yet in the haste of the moment, I picked out the Seven Smooth Stones that were to be sacrificed. Gingerly, apprehensively, and with tender loving care — and a prayer — I drew the stones, one by one, across that most sensitive of parts. I can truthfully state that this issue was solved without a tissue. But may Heaven help those whose stones are not smooth.

Where the ravine of interest to me opened up into the main canyon, there was a handsome family of blooming desert willows, not true willows but catalpas. They have drooping leaves, thin as a pencil lead, and a limp elegant flower of the palest lavender. The botanical name of this unusual tree is *Chilopsis*. It is one of those protected from the developer's bulldozer by the Scottsdale native plant ordinance (for which I'd worked).

The canyon I investigated for three hours was close-walled and of sandstone. Above it on the sharp inclines was a proud brigade of saguaros and above them rimrock of a deep mahogany hue. I found a swallow's nest, built surprisingly low, and could see in it four off-white eggs. Further up, I inadvertently terrified a horned lizard (better known as Ye Olde Horny Toad), sunning himself on a sandbar. He did a double-flip, careened around in circles, and finally escaped into a tangle of flood-debris.

This secluded place had its share of colourful birds which showed themselves to me. There was a hooded oriole, yellow and black, and those two red and feathered princes, the cardinal and the summer tanager. High aloft, soaring on a thermal current, was Old Zopilote, the scrawny-necked turkey vulture, watching me with the eye that missed nothing below.

On the way back I spotted an animal skull in the creek itself, entangled in algae. Pulling it free and scouring it with sand, I saw that it was a javelina's with a complete set of teeth and all four wicked curved tusks. It was the third I'd found during my years of desert roaming.

On the journey home — for home a base camp surely is in the back of beyond — had a surprise encounter with a big-horned, broad-headed bull taking the shade under a mesquite. Moving like the wind, I came and went so swiftly that he scarcely had time to register my presence. In all fairness to these fearsome fellows, I must say I've found the Arizona species to be docile. As a boy in England, my memories of bulls and bullocks are that they all charged on sight. But maybe that's because I was invariably trespassing on farmers' property.

My final evening was enhanced by the pinpointing of the whereabouts of a hooded oriole's nest. I'd seen this vivid pair, feathered in jet-black and yolk-yellow, flitting to and fro in the branches of the sycamore above me. But it wasn't till sunset of the last night that I located their hanging cup-nest camouflaged in the folds of a large leaf. A nice going-away present.

My mind was now dwelling on the long ascent out of the canyon — and the physical exertion it would demand. In order to make things easier on myself, I packed up everything possible before darkness fell. I filled the water jugs to the brim and set them to chill in the creek. The ashes and coals in the pit fire I crushed to a powder and then tamped six inches of damp sand on top of them. Dry sand was then smoothed over this, leaving not a trace of my kitchen area. I find whiteman's fire-rings, with a mound of ashes, charred logs, and smoke-blackened rocks, to be highly objectionable. The fine art of camping in the wilderness is to touch it as lightly and invisibly as a canyon breeze. And it becomes a matter of honour in doing so.

At twilight I made my heartfelt thanksgiving to the creek that had quenched my thirst and cooled my body, to the sycamore that had given me shade and fuel — and to the sand that had softened my bed. And in the tradition of the Bushmen of the Kalahari desert in southwest Africa, I gave my campsite the personal name of Place of the Hidden Nest Found.

Seventh & Final Day

> We are on the threshold of a new Revelation, a new awakening. But what we have accomplished up to this time must be multiplied a thousand-fold if the great battles are to be joined and won. Man must affirm his Spiritual Kinship with the Eternity of Nature.
>
> — Ansel Adams

Come the dawn and I was up with it, anxious to be off without delay. The first twittering of birds, Nature's salute to the new day, grew louder as I set about folding up the tent and rolling up the sleeping bag. By ten minutes to five, I was in harness and champing at the bit. A moment's pause for silent prayer, a soft-spoken *Adios* to the canyon encompassing me, and then I was off.

It was, quite simply, a race against the rising sun. The pressing need was to make the rim of the canyon before Old Sol was high enough to sap my energy and drain my water supply. And so it was all business now and I set a steady pace up a dry wash that I hoped would lead me to the saddle that I was searching for.

After a half hour of climbing gradually in the cool and shade of the early hour, I came out at the head of the gully which was in fact a shrub-covered saddle dividing two main watersheds. Looking at the rough and sharply rising terrain above me, I knew that whatever way I chose would be hit-and-miss as far as an accurate exit went. But I was sure of the general direction and was not lost. I came to a decision on the route out (which I later found out was a wrong one) and, now that I'd got my breath back, set off on the second stage.

Moments later I heard that now-familiar heavy sniff and snorting sounds in the chaparral. Another herd of javelina and again, undetected, I had the advantage. I kept still, listening and watching intently. Though they were all scattered like quail in the undergrowth, I waited till several showed themselves in a clearing. One burly male caught sight of me and began acting agitatedly — like a person in distress, pacing backwards and forwards. I now know that the fact I stay still and make no threatening motions puzzles them. They really don't know whether to flee or carry on with their munching.

As a rule, humans either hoot or shoot when they run into wild animals — and of course the animals have set responses to such predictable behavior. But what on earth does one do, as a self-respecting javelina, with a supposed enemy who neither hoots nor shoots and who even seems to be sending out good vibrations? When in doubt, head on out. Which is what most of them did. However, in their haste for self-preservation, they forgot to wake up a young one who was peacefully snoozing, with piggy eyes fully closed when I came upon him.

"Howdy, Junior!" I said cheerily, standing over him. He didn't stir. Was he sick? A second "Howdy!" brought him swiftly out of his sweet dreams. Up he sprang and off he dashed into the bushes. I imagined they'd all vanished until I heard a pathetic little squeal down in a hollow — and there, deserted by its mother, was a baby piglet so new to life that its eyes were still shut. I went up to it and saw that the poor thing was trembling with fright so I moved away quickly — fairly secure in the knowledge that the mother would seek out its defenceless baby as soon as I'd left the area.

Several years ago, I had a similar incident with an abandoned baby javelina. It strikes me as strange that the mother does not stand by its young in fierce defensive posture — as many other animals might.

Now began the gruelling half of the trek out of the canyon. The sun had lit up the mountainside but, still being early, its strength was subdued, thank God. Foot by foot, snatched at by the lacerating barbs of the cat-claw bushes, I slogged my way up that unforgiving slope. My heart was pounding like surf against my chest and I was wrapped around in the sour stench of sweat. But as I gasped and plodded upwards, shoulders bruised by the weight of the backpack, I could not help but marvel at the miracle of the body when taxed to the utmost. This brave frame had brought me — and forty-odd pounds more — 2,000 feet upwards over formidable ground that no mechanical invention could ever have begun to tackle. Even in the midst of the misery of sweat and gnats and strain, I exulted in the fullest use of this marvellous machine, my body.

In two hours and a quarter, after several wrong turns and winding detours, I arrived, tired but triumphant, at the high place that I had fought and sought for. In reaching the top, I did not think of my having conquered the mountain, I only thought of it having kindly cooperated with me. Men do not conquer mountains; mountains merely oblige men by letting themselves be climbed.

With a sense of profound gratefulness, I took one last lingering look at the splendid sweep of wilderness that had won my heart. Wilderness is no decent way to describe what had been so good and giving to me, I thought. And the words of

Chief Luther Standing Bear of the Oglala Sioux flooded into my consciousness at that moment:

> We Sioux did not think of the great open plains, the beautiful rolling hills, and winding streams with tangled growth as "wild" — only to the white man was nature a wilderness and only to him was the land "infested" with "wild" animals and "savage" people. To us it was tame. Earth was bountiful and we were surrounded with the blessings of the Great Mystery. Not until the hairy man from the East came and with brutal frenzy heaped injustices upon us and the families we loved was it "wild" for us. When the very animals of the forest began fleeing from his approach then it was for us that the "Wild West" began.

There is so much past and present grief in those words that I cannot bring myself to end these written words of mine in such a woeful way. Let me therefore finish the final day with Walt Whitman — as I began the first with him:

> Now I see the secret of the making of the best persons; it is to grow in the open air and eat and sleep with the Earth.

VI: El Desierto, Mi Amor: The Desert, My Love

September 8th to 14th 1984

First Day

Madrecita obliged me with two good omens just before I set out on this year's trek. In the dead of night before the day of departure, a herd of javelina came to munch on watercress in the creek directly below the cabin. Through the mists of half-consciousness, I heard them lunging about and grunting contentedly — but was too full of slumber to drag myself out of bed to look at them. Had they come also to wish me well on my wilderness foot-journey?

The second omen appeared in the slender shape of the resident rattler, RR. (I say *resident* because I believed this large black-tailed rattlesnake to be the same one I'd seen near the cabin on three separate occasions in the past month.) At the very moment of departure, Sioux (who had arrived in her truck) spotted him right at the place of stepping stones where I hop across the creek. With the deliberateness of one who knows just where he's going, RR slithered down the bank and bellied across the first boulder, staying dry. Then he swayed around a bit and dipped his underbelly in the water, feeling out the environment, as it were. Throwing caution to the desert winds, he proceeded to flop into the flowing creek, fully immersing his serpentine length before gaining the other bank. Sioux, with a better vantage point than me, reported that he emerged from the stream with his body straight as an arrow. Seeing me, he paused warily and then sensing no animosity or danger, continued up the rock floodwall toward the front of the cabin. It was as if he had shown up to stand guard on the canyon and the cabin in my absence. I saluted him thankfully.

Traditionally, Sioux has seen me off on these spells of solitary refinement, and so, again, she drove me a goodly distance to the place where I was to plunge into the wilderness. It was with a smile and a fond hug that we parted. Midmorning already — and the shimmering sun stood high in the scintillating September sky. The noise of her yellow truck *Abeja* (bee) faded away and I was alone once more, joyously alone, and in my ears the sounds of Nature, not of man.

A jay, flashing blue in the cover of juniper trees, welcomed me to the wilds with a harsh screech. The sun's heat pressed down on me, but I set a steady pace up a climbing rutted road and, even at the outset, knew what I had to do above all — find water.

I had not reconnoitered this area but assumed, from studying a map, that there would be a sufficiency of springs — if not some creek running miraculously through the hot desert. Actually it was not long before I passed by water, but it was a soupy, stagnating stock tank. Not too palatable, and scarcely potable, but it would do in an emergency. I made a mental note of it. The old jeep road I was plodding along showed little sign of use and a minimum of beer cans, which pleased me. My purpose was supreme and uninterrupted solitude. I was hellbent on removing myself as "far from the madding crowd" as possible. The road meandered much but I was happy to meander with it, having no set destination nor any whiteman's schedule to meet. After a while I came upon a fairly new and nastily obtrusive sign in red and white: MINING DANGER. Loathing the damage inflicted upon our public lands by mining, I was tempted to sabotage the sign but, instead, simply peed on it, a protest pee, in fact. One could say that I was able to let off steam in that fashion.

Then there came a fork in the road and I, "I took the road less travelled." This led me to a second stock tank, brimful of brackish water only a cow could enjoy. My own supply of water — a little more than two quarts — was adequate but it weighed me down. However, when wandering afoot through this land of little rain, I've always chosen to carry more water than perhaps necessary; for me that has proven a mental comfort as well as a bodily safeguard, well worth the sweat of the extra weight. Curiously, the first sweet and fresh water I found was inaccessible. I peered over the edge of a cliff at least a hundred feet high and could just make out a patch of water glistening in the sun far below. To reach it, down there in the box canyon amongst the leafy sycamore trees, would've called for a strenuous effort, but I was by no means desperate yet. Yet the sweeping isolated terrain did look dry and I was beginning to wonder whether, by the day's end, I'd be compelled to kneel down beside the range cattle and lap up the brown water at the stock tank.

Wild food there was aplenty. The prickly pear cacti were abundant and being the season so were their bursting-ripe purplish-red fruits. Brother Coyote, I noticed, had been making a meal of them; his scat, proudly plopped on wayside rocks, was thick with their pale-yellow seeds. What an opportunist that wild and wily canine is — he'll eat anything on Nature's bill of fare, be it animal, vegetable, or mineral. "God's dog," the Native Americans called him. To me, the coyote symbolizes freedom at its finest. He'll be around long after we've poisoned ourselves off this precious planet.

Up-and-down country this, ruled over by armies of junipers marching to the hazy horizons and all around them, lending support, Spanish bayonets of the yucca family. Now and then, on the lower slopes of the hills, I'd find myself bushwhacking through chaparral, a mean mix of scratching, snatching catclaw and prickly scrub oak. The stuff that curses and foul words were made for. (Wearing shorts makes me vulnerable in such situations. But I still prefer them to the sticky confinement of long pants.)

By mid-afternoon, sweating like the proverbial hog and stinking just as badly, I was craving a good campsite with water — and was glad to finally see, in the arroyo below, the dark-green crowns of sycamore trees. Like that tree of life, the cottonwood, sycamores too hold the promise of water. But, on reaching them, I was disappointed to find a dry stream-bed. It wasn't till half an hour later, after shedding my backpack and scouting a narrow side canyon, that — with vast relief and not a little gratitude — I happened upon a stand of slender stately cattails at whose base was a pool of shallow but cool, clear water. "*Gracias, Madrecita,*" I murmured in a prayer of thanksgiving. "You have never failed me yet...."

In this stretch of greenery, where the underground moisture had surfaced, grew tall yellow primroses and striking-scarlet cardinal flowers, and thick bunches of grass. A little Garden of Eden, no less. I lost no time in stripping to the skin and standing there, carefree as a wood-nymph, doused myself in water that took my breath away with its glorious coldness. How magically a desert spring can revive the aching body and flagging spirits. So I had discovered a home for a day or so. Before long my flimsy shelter, a tent of colours too awful to describe, was put up in a juniper clearing well above the creek's floodline. I relaxed and quickly unwound from the mental tension that mounts in a desert search for water.

Soon it was dinnertime. A small pit-fire, fuelled with aromatic juniper twigs, cooked me a meal of *machaca* — dried shredded beef, the perfect non-vegetarian backpacker's food —

and brown rice. This gourmet dish was swigged down with cowboy coffee. The light was failing as I crawled wearily but gratefully into the tent. Sleep was not slow in coming. It was, however, badly intruded upon by a blinding headache that struck at me in the middle of the moonlit night. Happily, by morning, it had ceased to torment me.

Second Day

Not wishing to be outdone by the astronauts, I enjoyed a cup of Tang for breakfast. The sugar in it had me buzzing round the campsite like an agitated bee. I spent the morning without a ponderous pack on my back, lightfootedly acquainting myself with the area. It was a pleasure to observe the lack of roads and to encounter nothing more of man's doings than old rusting barbed-wire fences and the occasional oxidized coffee can from another era. Not even hunters' shotgun shells and spent cartridges were to be seen. This was country that knew not the plague of people. As I gazed across its untrammelled expanses, I whispered this prayer, "God preserve this land from the ravages of man." It was enough the violence he had done to my beloved desert.

I climbed up out of the canyon and hiked in high places, following ridges and saddles and skirting rocky crags tinged with the redness of millenia. Animals there were few, though I did chance upon a shy rabbit, a briskly scurrying orange velvet ant (which both sting and squeak if picked up), and a sleepy garter snake whose only perceptible movement was the flickering of his inky-black forked tongue. Close above me, soaring free and searching for carrion, sailed a black vulture, an uncommon bird this side of the Mexican border where his red-necked relative, the turkey buzzard, predominates. Being lively meat too fresh for his deathly taste, I was ignored utterly, but nonetheless I greeted him with a friendly, *"¡Hóla, Zopilote!"*

Several times, once on a standing dead stick and then again on a sun-dried cowpie, I noticed the remarkable adobe work of desert termites. Because they cannot bear direct sunlight, they set about covering what they plan to eat with a layer of mud so they can do their chewing in darkness. Rather like gift-wrapping candy, I suppose. The gnats, damn 'em, were out in force, attacking my eyes and ears and heralding their onslaught with that horrid high-pitched whine. Only by keeping on the move is it possible to thwart their evil little designs. To swat them is to poke oneself in the eye or to get a self-inflicted thick ear. This summer particularly, they seemed to have multiplied maddeningly.

At the end of the morning, from up on a bluff, I spied a group of ranch buildings (seemingly unoccupied) down in a valley beside an arroyo. Decided to save them for a day later in the week. Retracing steps, with lunch in mind, I dropped back down into the canyon where my camp was and came upon a small shaded pool, hidden away in a grove of willows, sycamores, and cottonwoods, and cold as ice water compared to the inferno on open ground. Throwing off my grubby clothes, I slipped into the still water right up to my waist and then with a near-orgasmic "Aaaagh!" sank beneath the surface. "Blessed art thou," I breathed in ecstasy to the secret pool. No millionaire in chlorinated "Clearwater Hills" could ever hope to know the undiluted joy I was knowing then.

It had been a grand and vigorous morning and, despite slipping on loose earth and tumbling twice, I'd broken no limbs and had got safely back to base. With a lunch of bread and herring chunks stowed beneath my belt, I began the pleasing — and yet the tiresome — task of writing up this desert journal. To do so in reasonable comfort, I laid out a foam pad and a pillow at the base of a rough-barked juniper and, to foil the gnats, enshrouded my head in a piece of mosquito netting. I must have made a peculiar sight, like some derelict desert madonna. The nose-perching reading glasses sticking out from the green netting surely added to this bizarre effect. Today's writing was a four-hour stint.

While fetching water for supper, my thongs skidded on the grass tufts and I fell hard, bashing my right shin against a hidden rock. An ugly bump swelled up right away so I knelt in the pool, soaking the shin in cold water and then bound it with a wet bandanna. Nothing broken, thank Heavens — but it was quite painful. Supper did not vary from the previous night, nor would it for the rest of the trek. Brown rice, beefed up with *machaca,* dried chicken-and-rice soup made wet, a pair of cookies and a bowl of granola and powdered milk also made wet. This inspiring meal was helped down by the inevitable cups of strong black Mexican coffee.

An hour of daylight remained to me so, stubbornly refusing to have this time ruined by gnat attacks, I persevered through several pages of Poe and allowed old Edgar Allan to thoroughly scare me with one of his short stories. Later in the evening, unable to fall asleep, I lay on top of my sleeping bag and listened to the night cries of a great-horned owl and a poorwill, both so melancholy to human ears.

Third Day

Not the usual flawless sky this morning. There was a light cloud-cover which promised a greater build-up as the day went on. For me this meant cooler hiking so I was glad of it. Up earlier than yesterday, brewed myself a coffee before setting off on the morning's roamabout. I noticed, with regret, that already I'd trampled a plant here and a plant there. Calling to mind that Hopi saying, "Earth give life and seeks the one who walks gently upon it," I resolved to tread more carefully. Without plants, there would be no life on Earth and, besides, they have their destiny to fulfill as we do. However, man is a lumbering beast and it takes a special discipline on his part to walk gently upon the Earth.

This morning I followed the dry bed of a broad arroyo. Here and there were the light-green velvety mullein leaves from the centre of which shot up the straight and tall, slightly phallic seedstalk. This stalk, in olden days, because of its abrasive silicate make-up, was used as a pan-scourer. I passed by a twisting wild vine hung with midget bunches of purple-black grapes. They were sweet to the taste but large-seeded. Further down the winding, boulder-strewn course was a less palatable find, an old campsite strewn with food cans and sun-brittle plastic lids. It was far from recent trash, though, and that somehow reassured me. I willingly gave up ten minutes of my hiking day to scooping out a hole in the loose earth and burying the flattened cans. *Homo rapiens'* litter had no place in these wondrous wildlands.

I pressed on, relishing the cloudy coolness of the day, and upon rounding a bend, was treated to the sweetest surprise of all, trickling clear water. Praise be to thee, Madrecita! The bone-dry bed had ever so suddenly come wet-alive — and all manner of fresh green things were growing. I never cease to be entranced by the way in which desert water pops up in the driest of places and when least expected. To be given water (for it surely is a gift of Nature) out of the Great Blue is to be rid of the anxiety that lurks beneath the surface of the desert-wayfarer's mind. I walked on with a lighter heart — and came at last to a lovely spot where the cardinal flowers stretched in a floral colony for all of twenty feet along the creek's edge.

I stood transfixed by their blood-red brilliance.

Feeding on the nectar of these swaying scarlet petals were fluttering butterflies, blue, iridescent swallow-tails and a yellow-and-black tiger species whose wingspan must've been three inches. In the absorption of their feeding, of me they were unheeding.

Further on down I was stopped in my tracks by the discovery of a shrivelled deer-hide and antlers with the buck's skull still overlaid with skin. Wondered what ill luck had befallen that once-graceful animal. None but the hardiest of hunters would've penetrated this deep into the desert.

I was an hour out of camp by now and judged it time to climb out of the shaded canyon and push upwards to a prodigious piling of wind-smoothed sandstone boulders that overlooked the creek. Tumbled boulders, with their nooks and crannies, cracks and crevices, have always held a fascination for me and I simply couldn't pass them by without peering in and around them. Down below, to the left, ran another arroyo also full of the promise of water because of the gallery of sycamore trees lining it. Though, where water in the desert is concerned, seeing is believing. I made fair time, keeping to mid-slope and weaving in and out of the cactus patches and chaparral thickets — always with eyes peeled for rattlesnakes. For their sake and mine, I was not keen to step on them with a clumsy hiking boot and so was ever alert to that. Only a heavy foot on their back — nothing less than that, I'm convinced — might make them strike at one who meant them no harm. I despise those who slaughter them wantonly.

My desert dance was curtailed by an unavoidable passage through a green sea of low cat-claw bushes. "Wait a minute! Wait a minute!" they voicelessly signalled, sharply clutching at my skin and clothes. I got through this thorny barrier best by high-stepping rather than barging straight forward. Bloodied by gashes on arms and legs, had to remind myself that from this very same vicious bush came a superb desert honey. A massing of cat-claw such as that indicates severe overgrazing. Noteworthy, however, that I had not yet seen a single range-cow on this trip. That didn't bother me a bit since cows are both destructive and filthy creatures; there's no sorrier spectacle than trampled wild flowers along a creek or a sweetwater spring that's been fouled by cow-clap. Evidently I was indeed in cattle country because I hiked by a juniper-post corral, so long in disuse that a large bush grew in the centre of it and knee-high grasses choked its inner circle. For a long time no captive beast had bellowed there.

Beyond the corral, over a rugged rise, lay another creek with more riparian trees and a fine flow of water sparkling in the strong sunshine. Madrecita had proven more than bountiful to me — there was "water, water everywhere and *lots of* drops to drink." In a solid-rock stratum where the creek ran, there was a smooth hollowed-out basin of crystalline water. Submerged in it, I bathed away the caked blood and the sour sweat from my body. I swear that, for me, that had to be one of life's supreme sensations. Not only supreme, sublime.

This water-way I followed east and eventually, upon scrambling out of it onto higher ground, was startled by the sudden sound of big animals in the bush nearby. Cow? Deer? Javelina, perhaps? None of those — but horses! A pair of them loose, but not seemingly wild, here in the back of beyond. They kept their distance but watched me curiously. The mystery of their being there was part-solved by my coming upon an eroded and weed-filled track that led steeply to a cluster of simple ranch buildings. Probably little more than line-shacks used now and then by cowboys on cattle round-up. The entire property was thickly overgrown with tall weeds. A peek inside the main tin-roofed building revealed two rooms, one with iron bedsteads and stained sagging mattresses and the other with a handsome antique wood cooking stove beside which was a pile of recently-cut juniper logs. A dilapidated haybarn containing a metal box with GRANO (*grain* in English) painted on it, a bale of hay, and the skeleton of a skunk, was the only other structure save for a corrugated-iron outhouse.

The valley in which this neglected property sat was splendid in its natural surroundings and magnificent in its isolation. The fact that the ranch-house had not been vandalized in its abandonment attested to the remoteness of the region. I would've given my eye-teeth to own it! In getting to this place, I had hiked in a wide circle but still had my bearings thanks to yesterday's explorations. In short, I was not lost.

With high noon only an hour away, I began the long haul to the top of the ridge that would take me back to camp. A swift grey racer-snake slithered away from me in fright as I walked away from the old ranch. Yard by yard I gasped my way upwards, the sweat pouring from me, even though the sky by then was overcast. For all this exertion I knew it would've been worse in unshaded sunlight. At half-past the noon-hour I was back at the encampment, feeling famished.

Lunch consisted of a bread roll and a can of "bite-size" herring chunks, two cookies (yes, they were rationed), and several cups of hot tea. As with dinner, the luncheon menu varied not. Having hiked a full five hours, I was a little late in writing up the journal but managed to record most of the day's adventures before rain made me hastily put pen and paper away. The blackening clouds had been flexing their muscles all day long. By late afternoon they meant business.

At first the rain was light enough to allow me a cooking fire and good enough to drive off the nattering gnats. I was grateful therefore for a hot meal, even if I was a trifle frantic in its preparation. By six o'clock there were flashes of lightning and growling thunder — and I was battening down the hatches of the tent, expecting the worst. The storm was unusually prolonged. It gave battle directly above my frail shelter with mighty thunderclaps and electrifying light displays — and it rained like hell. My poor, aging little tent which had done sterling service in such unlikely places as the Yorkshire moors, the Mexican Sierra Madre, and the Icelandic glaciers, would have been flooded out but for a broad plastic sheet draped over it. That sheet used to be a tube tent till I slit it down the middle.

I did not sleep during this commotion but stayed reasonably dry, and that's a blessing in the wilds. The rain beat a tattoo on the plastic tarp, stopped and then started up again, three times in all. I was snug but not smug. Hard to be the latter with metal tent-poles and lightning leaping all around. After two hours or more, the storm abated and all fell silent again.

It seemed forever before I got to sleep.

Fourth Day

Close to an inch of rain had dropped into my coffee cup by the campfire. It had been quite a storm. But now the thirsty earth had drunk its fill and the morning air smelled sweet and cleansed. I needed to lay scent again so, like a dog who rations his pee to better mark his territory, I strategically piddled around the boundaries of the campsite. I may've seemed like a silly-willy in doing this, but actually it served to alert roaming animals to my own territorial claims.

Before setting forth on the morning hike, I found out that a gnat or two had infiltrated that holiest of holies, the inside of the tent. This infuriated me. I wanted revenge for all the unceasing misery visited on me by these wretched insects. So I took a smoking juniper twig from the breakfast fire, gleefully set it in a saucepan, stuck it inside the tent doorway, and fastened down the flaps. Since the invading gnats were too tiny to choke to death, I simply smoked them to death. So much for my reverence for that particular form of life. As the smoke gently billowed out from beneath the flaps, I remembered having left my sleeping bag in the tent, and smiled ruefully. Well, I thought to myself, I've heard of smoked salmon before, but never of smoked sleeping bag.

This morning turned out to be a mixture of path-finding and trail-blazing. I had a rough idea of the direction I'd need to take to get home to the cabin but I was not sure how accessible or broken the way would be. Again, without the deadweight of a backpack, I did some reconnoitering. The ascending ravine that I looked into was like a mad giant's staircase made up of great boulders that he had flung haphazardly down from a mesa-top. I scrambled up this zany staircase, heaving myself up over the colossal boulders and snapping off dead branches wherever they hindered passage. The only wildlife I saw was a wee rock-hopping wren and three lithe garter-snakes who were surprised to see me. There were pools of muddy water left over from last night's downpour. I wondered if they would be clear and potable by the time me and my backpack came that way.

Higher up, the ravine became a mere gully which itself merged into the flatness of the mesa top. The panorama below and around me—a superb circular sweep—was awe-inspiring. I chose to take this exploratory route on the day of departure; it had been worth the scouting endeavour. Much, much easier the descent — pleasure, not work — and I did more than rock-hop, I boulder-bounced my way down. At lower elevation, sycamore trees closed in the canyon and there was so much moisture in that sunless air that moss grew thick and tight-packed on the bigger boulders wedged in the tinkling creek. I regained the main streambed, dipped deliciously in a wayside pool, and turned campwards with lunch uppermost in my thoughts. Made one short stop to pick a pocketful of wild grapes, dessert courtesy of Mother Nature.

Before the deep cutoff to my side canyon, I wandered through a stand of sunflowers, some prime and pretty specimens a good foot taller than me. They had chosen the creek-bed to live out their summer lives and had had luck since no flashflood had come to tear them down. There were red tubular honeysuckle flowers, too, being wooed by the thrusting long-bills of vivacious hummingbirds. It surprised me to see that none of the arroyos had flooded overnight. I would have thought it inevitable after an entire inch of sharp rainfall. Yet my desert is full of surprises, never as mundane as man.

On the last stretch, up the narrow gulch sliced out of red earth, I spotted large tracks in the slick orange mud and first thought, A cow, damn it! Closer inspection showed not a hoof mark but a cat's paw as wide and deep as my clenched and flattened fist. In the four short hours that I'd been away from camp, I had had a regal visitor in my desert place, a mountain lion. It was thrill enough just to know that without ever laying eyes on it. But I did keep my eyes wide open. Once upon a time, seven years before, in the Sierra Madre, my friend Michael Rhye and I had the extraordinary and exquisite experience of seeing a pride of five or six mountain lions springing up a canyonside in broad daylight. Incredible.

I was anxious to be back at camp because of an early gathering of more rain clouds and because I'd left my sleeping bag out, draped over a fallen trunk. I could've easily coped with a smoked sleeping bag but not with a smoked and sodden one. As it happened, Old Sol did an amazing job of burning off the mass of moisture in the heavens and by late afternoon, in spite of a slight drizzle, had thoroughly dispersed each black cloud.

Not wanting to have to huddle inside the tent to continue writing, I was thankful for this — and said so to the sun.

By mid-afternoon I was up to date on the journal and made the decision to strike camp and move to a less constricted area where there was ample water and even a skinnydippery. I pounded the wood ashes in the pit-fire to grey powder and covered them with damp earth and a layer of juniper needles. Scattered the pile of firewood over the flattened ground of the tent-site and gave thanks to this spot that had cared for me for a few days. I knew that the next rainfall would eliminate all trace of my ever having been there. And that is exactly as it should be with man or woman in the wilderness.

Was the mountain lion watching me from a brushy lair as I walked off? That I shall never know.

A half-hour's leisurely hiking brought me to my new home in the outback. The site I had picked could well have been sacred, so I entered reverently. It was a druid's grove of curving ash trees on a wooded embankment safely above creek-level. The spot beneath which I pitched the tent was roofed over by nine ash trunks rising from a tight cluster. Nearby were four more, to add to this curious arboreal grouping. I had superior shade and firewood aplenty. With the setting up of new camp, I was late in cooking dinner, and by the time the last bitter brew of *Café Combate* had gone down my gullet, darkness had closed in on my sylvan sanctuary. Stretched out on my back inside the tent, I heard the crickets' orchestra strike up and, hoping to stay awake for the rising of the full moon, I listened for a while — with a smile — to their mad monotone melodies.

Yes, I did see the full moon in all her silvery majesty — but later in the night and through sleep-clogged eyes and the tent's flyscreen.

Fifth Day

There was the nip of autumn in the air early this morning and I found myself hunching, like an Indian, over the tiny coffee-fire to absorb its warmth. The purpose of today's side-hike was to determine just how isolated this area was; in other words, to be on the lookout for litter, footprints, and encroaching roads, if any. An ear tuned to the noise of vehicles, however distant, would also assist in this investigating. God knows, there was noise enough aloft, with commercial and private 'plane traffic, screaming air force jets and thwack-thwacking military helicopters. One of the singular joys of the Mexican backcountry is the silence and sanctity of its skies. Thoreau once wrote, "Thank God man cannot lay waste to the skies as he has the earth." Poor man would turn in his urn if he knew how man had interfered with the heavens.

By keeping to the creek's course and out of the upper chaparral all morning, I gave myself an easy time of it. It was a gentle and agreeable experience and, because of that, I was prone to observe more closely the natural goings-on. Slogging up a slope thick with bristly bushes was not conducive to the poetic appreciation of Nature. Wildlife sightings were again of the small kind — a great-horned owl flushed from its daytime dozing, a ground squirrel sprinting for safety up a crumbling bank, an orange-winged blueblack-bodied tarantula hawk scurrying through the dead leaves in busy search of her spider prey, a bevy of butterflies (six species, at least, I counted) sipping on the blooms that were there only because of the trickling creek. The grasshoppers feasting on the sunflower heads and catapulting themselves out of my path, those strange and skillful insects that devour sycamore leaves and having done their work, wrap themselves in a leaf cocoon and then slide down to earth on a single silken thread of their own making, and a showy red summer tanager (still here in early fall) with its *Pity-chuck! Pity-chuck!* call. During this ramble I also chanced upon a giant water bug, but this unfortunate's pool must've dried up on him since he was trekking along a part of the streambed that was dry as dust. Although amphibian in nature, he looked to be in desperate straits without a pool to paddle in so, rather fruitlessly, I must admit, I tipped the contents of a full water-canteen over him.

The giant water bug, with its biting and sucking mouthparts, is the very devil himself for other aquatic life in desert creeks. He's also quite the lover, it seems. The male I spotted today was carrying on his back an overload of eggs. Apparently to ensure better protection against predators for those eggs, he persuades the female to lay them not just anywhere, but specifically on his back. She must stick them on with a dab of Elmer's waterproof because they stay glued on tight till they hatch. The catch is that for every egg she lays, he lays her. And there were one hell of a lot of eggs on that brute's back! To put it in more scientific terms, every time he copulates, she populates. *Muy, muy macho,* that *cucaracho.* With a fellow like that around, one has to be pretty cautious when skinny-dipping in creeks. One's family jewels could be in serious jeopardy. All I know is that I wouldn't want his biting and sucking mouthparts latching onto any of my parts.

Two hours of hiking convinced me of how perfectly sequestered this stretch was. I did come across a few pieces of trash but none of them recent. Even by climbing high, I could make out no roads intruding upon the region and I saw no footprints but my own. Mine were few and far between since nowadays I tend to walk in the Indian manner and in the discipline of trying to leave no tracks. Snakes, however, cannot practise this human discipline. One roving reptile had left an odd keyhole-shaped body-mark in the soft sand.

On the juniper-dotted hillsides rising above the riparian way, there were gigantic groupings of yellowstone boulders, some perched precipitously on top of others and, at the end of the first half of the morning's foot journey, there to greet me with upstretched arms and classic countenance, stood a saguaro cactus at the foot of one of these tremendous blocks of rock. It was the first saguaro of the trip and therefore significant to me.

Before heading back, a prickly pear cactus caught my attention. It was so laden with smooth-skinned, pregnant-plump purple fruit that I simply had to pick one for the camp larder. It could not be painlessly removed from the plant without first having its glochids cut off. Glochids are the tiny hair-like spines that play hell with the fingers, tongue, and lips. I scraped them off with a sharp knife.

I must've set a cracking pace on the way back because I was at camp by eleven o'clock, just seconds too late to get a glimpse of what I suspect were javelina bolting into the tangled undergrowth above the creek. Lots of narrow cloven hoofprints in the moist sand below. This extra hour of non-hiking time before noon encouraged me to do some chores — the washing of a revoltingly smelly tee-shirt, some drawers that weren't quite that bad, and a pair of sticker-infested socks, then the shampooing of my golden locks that had gone gritty and dust-brown. All the soaping and lathering was done well out of range of the crystal-clear creekwater; a plastic gallon jug, modified for this purpose, helped with these outdoor ablutions. With all this cleanliness over and done with, I sat upon a weathered log and reflected on my good fortune at being in this place of tranquillity.

The most modest of rattles drew my eye over to another fallen limb and there, once more, was my old friend *Crotalus*, a black-tailed rattlesnake seeking out a shady spot to while away the afternoon. All I could discern was a pale yellow rattle held up in the air by a charcoal-coloured tail. The triangular head and the bulk of the body had insinuated itself under a carpet of leaves. I wished this peaceful snake a pleasant siesta. Beyond count now are the number of meetings I've had with rattlesnakes in the wild. It has been my privilege, at various times, to see them sleeping and very much awake, angry and upset but much more often peaceful, drinking at streams and eating their kill — and even making love. I have been honoured to observe them under many and differing circumstances. I respect them because they have respected me. I envy them because they are closer to the earth than me. I like them because they have taught me much and so, whenever I am given the opportunity to protect them from harm, I seize it. In spite of their potent venom, they are not the malicious creatures that *Homo rapiens* makes them out to be — and should always be relocated rather than killed. Long live Old Crotalus, I say!

Sitting with my black pen in hand and my back to a conveniently leaning juniper, I wrote up the journal and now and then gazed up at the caravan of cumulus clouds drifting by. It was a radiant day, with perfect temperatures, and I relished every moment of it. At the risk of sounding repetitious, I'm going to mention the gnats again because, in truth, they were the only odious aspect of the entire experience. If I ever had a daughter, I would under no circumstances name her Natalie. After an especially bad gnat-tack, I began to wonder what an appropriate collective noun for these pesky insects would be. So I put on my thinking cap and these are what I came up with: a nagging of gnats, a nirritation of gnats, a 'nnoying of gnats, and a 'naggravation of gnats. I did have some success with fresh garlic as a repellent; there was a drawback to it, though, a stinging sensation around the eyes and ears where it had been rubbed in. Even worse when the garlic juice got into the eye.

Had a minor ocular emergency when the left support-piece of my reading (and writing) glasses dropped off during this afternoon's scribbling session. With only one wing, so to speak, the glasses kept falling off and I ended up having to wear a bandanna headband in which to wedge the other. One has to improvise in the wilderness; there is, after all, no Circle K convenience store just around the creek-bend. (Thank God!)

I was finished with writing early enough in the afternoon to take a short walk — and was puzzled to come upon a sycamore tree whose great-girthed trunk was decorated with a series of cow bones wired together to form some unreadable initials, I supposed. They had been there for many a year and some were broken in two. The handiwork of range cowboys, I guessed.

Night had fallen by the time I was done with dinner. I slipped into the tent, full of gratefulness for yet another day of delight and discovery.

Sixth Day

Time galloping by with the speed of a race-horse. So many secret places yet to explore and with only one day left to me. I began wishing that I'd started out on this trek a day earlier — or maybe a year earlier. Not possible to extend it because neighbour David was expecting me back not later than tomorrow night — and he had clear instructions to notify the county sheriff's office if I did not appear by then. Seize this day therefore — and extract its essence!

With packed lunch in shoulder bag, I was on the move by 7 a.m. and today, this last day before heading home, I was set to roam for a good seven hours before returning to write. This journal has been a chain around my legs because it has to be written up daily, here and now, or it will never be written at all. I know that, and must discipline myself to that knowledge. But I know also that, afterwards, its completion as a record of a wilderness adventure will give lasting pleasure to me and possibly to others.

The game is worth the candle, as the old saying goes.

I took off up a side-canyon, one that had water in it and reddish sand. It started to look familiar. I realized that I'd been up it before, that it led to the abandoned ranch. But I kept going, never bored with beauty seen a second time. Passed the ranch-site and was disgusted to notice the trash that had been tipped over the creek-bank behind the buildings. The owners or the users had been too idle to haul it out — but then it'd been my experience that ranches and rubbish sometimes went together.

The water did not fail in this hemmed-in canyon but I didn't follow it to its source. Rather, I turned about and sought out a gully by which I could climb up to the highlands. This gully became quickly entangled with overhanging vegetation so, with shepherd crook Horace's stout assistance, I picked my way up a treacherous loose-gravel incline. Getting to the top of this ridge was an energetic enterprise but once there I stumbled on a disused pack-trail that became less and less visible as it wandered downwards. A couple of rusting discarded old horse-shoes told a horseman's tale of long ago.

The trail vanished into flaxen grass on the lower slopes but, by then, a weather-beaten cabin of stone and sheet iron had come into view. Old unlived-in cabins are always fascinating — what stories and histories they must have. Who on Earth would choose to live out their lives in this far-off place so removed from other human beings? Someone like me, perhaps. The wild grasses had grown tall all around it and up through an iron bedstead that sat outside, exposed to wind and rain. Inside this humble abode, no larger than 12x15 feet, there was a rock-hearth and fireplace, a crude wooden table, and a bench for two. An empty brandy bottle of ancient vintage stood forlornly on the table and there were dusty glass jars and bent pan lids on crooked shelves. The only living occupants were two scorpions who scuttled off in fright as I lifted up the yellowing newspaper that had concealed them. There were debris and dirt on the cement floor and bullet-holes in the tin roof. The cabin bore the sadness of all dwelling places bereft of care and love. I went out into the smiling sunshine, the friendly desert, and walked away from this sadness and desolation.

I took to following the twisting course of the low-flowing creek which ran below the cabin. All of an hour went by before I refound my bearings. There is nothing alarming about being slightly lost in the desert when beneath one's feet are rocks gleaming with the wetness of water. A racer-snake sped away from me so swiftly that I caught a glimpse of only its rear end as it shot into the brush. The sight of a six-inch centipede, orange-yellow with black cross-stripes and a pair of frenziedly-waving feelers, gave me pause for a few moments — long enough for the stunning revelation that a centipede is in fact a "fortypede." This I know because I counted each pede — and there were twenty to each side of its wriggling body. It got itself in a huff, became an incensedipede, and took a poisonous peck at poor Horace before squirming to safety in the cleft of a rock.

On the last leg, when I was growing weary and a bit footsore, two favourite birds of the region showed themselves to me. Phainopepla, the crested silky-flycatcher (a black beauty, to be sure) and another catcher of flies, this one with a black head, the streamside phoebe. This past spring I had a pair of phoebes build a cozy nest of mud and twigs on the wall of my cabin under the eaves.

Made it back to camp just ten minutes short of my projected seven-hour stomp — and celebrated with a cooling dip and two cups of tea. I've had to be watchful with my tea and coffee-water for when I've filled the canteens from the spring aquatic bugs have been sucked into their openings. Most distressful for the hapless bug to be in plasticized captivity and not especially beneficial for me since I was getting quite enough protein from the lunch sardines. I've made several efforts to return each frantic captive to its water environment. Jacques Cousteau and Albert Schweitzer would be proud of me. If by mischance I have swallowed any, then I've not felt the worse for it.

This afternoon, again, Old Sol chased away the assembling clouds with his fiery breath and I was left to write outside in unsprinkled peace. *Mañana* I shall rise at first light and strike out for home. Before retiring, I made as ready as possible for the early morning take-off. Filled in the fire-pit and camouflaged it over with leaves and twigs, topped up all the canteens (for water, tomorrow, was an unknown quantity and I needed to carry with me all I could) and packed for the most part.

I didn't sleep well that last night. In fact, I never have slept soundly in the out-of-doors. This is strange since one would anticipate the deepest and purest of sleep after daily hiking in the fresh, clean, and open air. I'm not afraid of animal visitors in the night, so it's nothing psychological. But I don't worry about this tossing and turning any more, merely accept it as a small price to pay for the overall elemental experience.

I heard the twittering of an elf-owl before finally slipping into sleep.

Seventh and Final Day

My natural alarm went off at daybreak. It was simply the chirping of the proverbial early bird out and about getting his worm. There's always a sense of urgency to any morning of departure. This one was no exception. I was not assured of drinking water in the uplands and so the sooner I could climb out of the canyon on to high, even terrain, the more bodily moisture would be conserved. Getting to the top before the sun could reach me would be invaluable help in this. Thus I made haste and was packed and ready within half an hour. Despite the pressure of the moment, I did not fail to thank my druid's grove of ash trees for their hospitableness — and gave a hearty hug to two of the nine trunks. I then straightened up a sorry-looking seedling that had been bent over by my tent's sitting on it, and watered it in compensation.

¡Adelante, caminante! No hay camino. Se hace camino al andar! (Onward, traveller! There is no path. The path is made by walking.) I came to the mouth of the gully leading upwards and began the ascent. The air was cool and I was rested — and had strength of purpose. Surely, steadily I worked my way over and around each lichen-covered boulder that stood in the path. Up, up, up. The climb seemed interminable and yet I was still in solid shade. In the final steepness, I was pulling and pushing myself up this massive stairway, sometimes on hands and knees. The backpack was a millstone upon my body. Once I lost my balance and unwittingly flung Horace onto a lower boulder.

"Solace! Horace," I said, grinning in spite of myself, "we're getting there." And, *poco a poco*, we were. Coming upon a *tinaja*, a hollowed rock filled with rainwater, I splashed my face and wet Horace's handle. The gully turned toward the east, narrowed, traded its monolithic rocks for just ordinary ones, and began to even out. After exactly one hour of heavy hiking, I was almost to the rim of the mesa when all of a sudden, lo and behold, the sun struck the head of the gully and illumined all with its bright white light. Dear Old Sol had been born again, yet again, to shine warmth and life on our little corner of the planet. I stepped over the last rise, dropped my pack on the ground, turned to face the great glowing orb in his kingdom of purest blue and with arms outstretched and raised high, I cried, "*¡Buenos dias, Sol! Te quiero mucho.*" (Good day, Sun! I love you.)

I caught my breath for five minutes, quenched the thirst from the climb, shouldered the pack, and set off into the sun. Within no time at all, a "Look at that!" escaped my lips. There in the yellow-blooming snakeweed lay a five-point rack of antlers still attached to a skull half bleached, half covered in hide. It had doubtless been a lion-kill and was now to be my prize. The distance between the tips of each antler measured seventeen inches. For miles across the mesa-top I hand-carried it but came to find that irksome and so lashed it with rope to the backpack.

Mesa-tops are their own unique experience. They make for mild hiking since they rarely possess much vegetation or rocky obstacles — and are as flat as any land in this great Sonoran desert of ours. Take away the odd juniper that grows there and they have a semblance of bleak (but beauteous) Yorkshire moorland to them. The prolific snakeweed could be the heather of the moors and the clumps of beargrass the bracken of my native heath. On a day of cold, damp, rolling mist there'd be no knowing the difference. Mesas are, in essence, land-bound islands suspended high in the desert air — and there's a grandeur in their unpeopled loneliness. The only water up there was of a dubious quality in artificial ponds created in catchment areas by ranchers for their cattle. Drinkable if boiled or treated, no doubt, but less than palatable after clear creekwater.

Yes, cattle were lumbering about on the mesa. I supposed that they and I would be the only living creatures in that lofty place. I was wrong. During almost four hours of skywalking, I saw all kinds of wildlife: coveys of twittering quail, a bounding jack-rabbit, a sun-sleepy bullsnake, ants building castles in the soft earth, and a cawing raven that flew across the face of the still-visible day-moon and seemed, for an instant, strangely supernatural. "Nevermore!" quoth I to the winging raven, but he croaked naught back.

My path had led me to a scarcely discernible rancher's track that serviced the stock-tanks. I kept to it, judging that it would bring me at last to the highway. As a precaution, I filled a smaller canteen (by then empty) with the silted brown-water of a cow-pond, planning to drink it only in dire need. The mesa stretched on endlessly, much further than imagined. I wondered if I would ever come down off it. Or was I doomed, like the Flying Dutchman, to roam forever? Madrecita, evidently, could not let me end this trek without showing me at least some of her larger wild children. In mid-morning, at a distance, I sighted five delicate deer, all does, prancing away from me through the low vegetation. This then was my ultimate treat, for it was not long after that the faint track began to drop down the curved side of the plateau. I knew where I was, and below the ribbon of road sought beckoned me. I set foot on it three and three-quarter hours after starting out on the journey at sun-up. From then on it was the open road and familiar stuff, yet I was still five hours away from home.

Old Sol was by now high in the sky and bearing down on me like a furnace but I was in fine spirits and trudged on uncomplaining. The first human being I ran into was, unfortunately, a youth on a dirt-bike. He nodded at me through the anonymity of his space helmet (I assume it was a he) and I scowled back at him. No lover of dirt-bikes am I. They are rippers of the earth and killers of its silences.

Marched on till high noon. Heat and exertion were taking their toll on me. I made straight for a source of flowing water, already known of. Upon reaching it at last, I let drop my pack and collapsed backwards on the ground, not so much in a dead faint as in utter relief from the physical output of the day.

Ah, the overwhelming joy felt upon flinging my tired and aching body into that precious pool. I splashed and gambolled around with the exuberance of a child and the addedappreciation of a grown man. The rushing water to me, at that moment, was nothing less than a miracle in motion. "This is even better than sex!" I exclaimed. All things are relative and it occurs to me that we have to experience extremes to become aware of the true value of something (or someone, for that matter).

In that intense moment I *knew* the immeasurable value of water in the desert.

For three hours during the hottest part of the day, I rested and wrote. And I had just three more hours of foot-slogging ahead of me. Storm clouds had marshalled in the afternoon sky and, mercifully, I got on my way again under cooling conditions. How the last leg of any journey drags out! And yet the fatigue and drudgery of it for me were mitigated by the loveliest of all sky-sights, a rainbow. This luminous arc-of-many-colours was broken in its middle by a billowing of black clouds from which fell a sheet of grey rain. Being on foot, I was able to watch its celestial prime and evanescence in a way I never could have done confined in a car. This heavenly radiance I looked upon as Madrecita's going-away gift to me. And as if to complement the ethereal with the earthy, a collared snake — drab-coloured on its upper body and vivid orange on its underside — crossed my ending path.

The rainbow and the snake were perfect parts of the great glorious whole.

As the sun, this day, had risen upon my setting forth so it was sinking upon my journey's end. I had been travelling for nine hours and I gave a prayer of devout thanksgiving to God and Madrecita for the surefootedness and strength-of-purpose that had brought me safely home.

In this journal I have been a singer of the desert's praises. If by some this song has been heard with sympathy then I have achieved what I aspired to do.

VII: Soledad, Serenidad: Solitude, Serenity

Monday August 3rd — Sunday August 9th 1987

Sleeping soundly through a tearing tempest has never been my custom. The night before the start of this trek, I retired to bed early with a four a.m. wake-up in mind. At eleven p.m. a summer storm rent the still of the night and stabbed the blackness of my canyon with spears of lightning. Madrecita was angry, her tears of rage fell fiercely. She didn't calm down till the early hours. Four o'clock came all too quickly — and I felt fatigued before I'd even begun my backpack. I was to meet my friend Tom S— up on the high road at five a.m. but, as he wasn't there, I pressed on to his cabin. A *"Buenos dias, Tomás!"* called up to his bedroom window got a quick response — and it wasn't long before we were in his car (backpack and all) and on the road to my trailhead.

We were privileged to witness the rising of the sun in the cloud-topped mountains to the east. I remembered Henry David Thoreau's words:

> It is true, I never assisted the sun materially in his rising; but doubt not, it was of the last importance only to be present at it.

It was just after six a.m. when I baled out of Tom's car, thanked him for his kindness, shook hands, and cut into the wildland. There wasn't a soul for miles around — and all was quiet — the sort of quietude that only Madrecita, Mother Nature, can give. It was precisely what I wanted — solitude and silence.

I set a course for the lowest point in a craggy range that lay to the north of a brooding mesa. Passed thro' a "prescribed burn" area and though the fire was long dead, my nose could still pick up the acrid smell of burnt earth. These controlled burns, visibly so devastating, are often carried out at the request of ranchers who dislike the dense chaparral that chokes out their cattle's forage. The irony of this is that the "noxious" plants, such as catclaw, prickly pear, and scrub oak, have dug themselves in precisely because of overgrazing by cattle. Cows are anathema to public lands — and should be wholly removed.

Angling across the desert, dipping down into narrow arroyos and climbing out by way of juniper-dotted ridges, I came finally to an old track servicing a stock-tank. This I began to recognize from a footjourney two years ago. It led me windingly to a pass between mountain and mesa. Along the way, going my way, was a high-stepping tarantula, a sole male in search of a female in her burrow. It is the males that wander — and especially at this time of year. Their two front legs, furry and jointed, have a spur apiece, used to lock onto the female during mating. I wonder if that's where the term *to be spurred on* comes from? Anyhow, to make myself more intimately known to this spider-wayfarer, I laid an open hand right in his path. He half-climbed onto it but then thought better of it and stepped back onto the road. Contrary to wrong impressions given by James Bond movies and the like, tarantulas are the gentlest creatures and will bite only under severe provocation. And even then the bite is mild.

Blue jays, dashing but noisy fellows, were out and about in their favourite trees, the junipers. They always set up such a chattering racket when they spot human intruders.

Ascending the long sandy slope, I found the going harder than usual. The backpack, with a full seven days of food and two half-gallon containers of water, weighed a ton. Well, not exactly, more like forty-five to fifty pounds. But that was heavier than I was used to. Besides, with little sleep the night before, I was tiring quickly. Added to that was the high humidity. Looking skywards I could see the rainclouds gathering again — but hardly had to worry about being soaked with rain. I was already sodden with sweat.

My way was blocked twice by barbed-wire fences over which, awkwardly, I had to hoist the backpack. It was a leaden load. Once, a shoulder strap came loose but I managed to jury-rig it with a piece of wire from the rancher's fence. For the first time ever, I'd brought along a small pair of pliers — and was damned glad of it!

Now high up on a flat, open piece of land, I noticed four species of hedgehog cactus (*mammillaria*), the most striking being a tightly-packed "colony" of claretcup cacti. This many-headed clump was more than a yard in length and the same in width. Imagine what a splendid sight when flowering. My desert rat amigo Cactus Jim once referred to this communal cactus as "Mother of a hundred." An apt name, in this instance, since there must've been close to a hundred in the clump.

I dropped down into a dry and rocky wash which stayed that way for much too long. It was water I wanted to see. Without it, I would have to make a forced march back — and did not relish that prospect. Sycamores and some cottonwood trees pointed to sub-surface water — but that wouldn't do me much good. I came to a spring at last, glory be! Yet it wasn't as clear or as free-flowing as I remembered it. Downcreek a little way it improved and looked drinkable. So, flagging from the four hours of hiking, I lost no time in unshouldering that blooming backpack and setting up camp. Even before the tent was fully up, I gave into my tiredness and took a siesta, sprawled naked as a babe on the blue nylon.

The campsite was friendly and familiar to me, a druid's grove of ash trees, packed closely together in a cluster of ten outwardly-leaning trunks. I hugged them hello. I say, if you meet a tree, hug it. If you greet a lizard, kiss it. In the bushes just beyond the grove was a one-fanged javelina skull, which I took as a sign of Madrecita's welcome.

Lunch was predictable — and was to be so for the next seven days. Brown bread, sardines, fresh garlic (to keep away the humans), an apple, fig bars, and almond herbal tea. A rainfall, not too severe, sent me into the tent which, even without fly sheet, kept me and mine fairly dry. I got comfortable inside and for about half an hour while the rain fell, read choice horror stories in preparation for my annual Halloween reading. With the rain soon over, I emerged and, sitting on a rough-barked moss-painted log, wrote up this journal for two hours. A phainopepla and I entertained each other by swapping bird calls.

Dinner was what dinner always is when on a desert roamabout — boiled brown rice and chopped up vienna sausages — with cookies for dessert — and cowboy coffee to wash it all down. This camping diet scarcely varies and though deadly dull, it does permit me to shop easily for a trek such as this.

The evening's diversion was entirely unexpected and every bit as good as television. Flickering fireflies, many of them, along the creekbed and always close to the water — and performing a sort of luminous airborne ballet in and out of the reeds. Before crawling into the tent at nightfall, I admired a stand of long-stemmed yellow evening primroses whose buds had once opened into flower before my very eyes on a previous solo. I knew their blossoming life to be only the length of one night. They would wilt and wither in the morning sun.

Despite overcast skies, the waxing moon was able to make her hazy appearance upon the retiring of the sun. This night, with no energy to read by candlelight in the tent, I slept the sleep of the exhausted.

Second Day

> The wild requires that we learn the terrain, nod to all the plants and animals and birds, ford the streams and cross the ridges, and tell a good story when we get back home.
>
> — Gary Snyder, *The Practice of the Wild*. Essays, 1991

I was up at six a.m. and, within an hour, ready for a stint of side-hiking. With a packed lunch and drinking water in my knapsack, I had in mind to follow the course of the creekbed for as far as it would take me. Needed to confirm that I was indeed well and truly isolated from my fellow man. Taking a deep drink at the waterhole before setting out, I surprised a platoon of bombardier beetles who scurried off (or, more appropriately, beetled off) in all directions. These blue and orange insects have the rare ability to shoot a puff of whitish chemical vapour from their backends when touched. Imagine! A backside with a built-in bomb! And there's actually a popping sound that goes with the launching of their bombs.

The first stretch of the creek walk was lush, damp, and shaded, giving moist habitat for grasses, marsh reeds, cattails, some sunflowers even. Here and there was a furry-leafed mullein with its rather phallic stalk that somehow got it the common name of horse's tail. Occasional pools of water hemmed in by flood-polished boulders made happy homes for suction-footed canyon tree frogs — and I saw a number of their young ones clinging to creekside crevices. Above me a pair of zone-tails created a hawkish hullabaloo as I passed underneath their deep nest of twigs and small branches high up in a cottonwood tree. How they shrieked their disapproval of me, wheeling and wailing above the canyon tree-tops. The pungent smell of skunk wrinkled my nostrils at one point, but I saw neither hide nor hair of the animal. I was glad to find no footprints, no shotgun shells, nor any trace of human activity, but I did run into cows further on. Where there are cattle there must sooner or later be cowboys. At the end of this creekwalk (three hours one way) I came across an old line-shack, little more than a wooden frame with squares of green tin sheets nailed to it. Peeking inside the cob-webbed gloom, I made out the usual spring beds, cast-iron stove, rusting skillet, and cracked enamel coffee pot. Though it hadn't been made use of by cowboys on roundup for years, there was an unsightly spilling of recent trash from an overturned garbage can outside. This mess, so jarring to the unspoilt natural surroundings, I cleaned up and put back in the garbage can. The can I then stowed inside the shack — and on top of it left a chiding and rather rude note for the rancher and his cowhands. The latter — and litter — seem to go together. (Maybe it is not macho to pick up beer cans so "masculinely" tossed away?) Satisfied to know that a healthy chunk of wild and dry land lay between my camp and the nearest jeep track to civilization (a misnomer, indeed), I turned about and trudged back to base along the meandering and rockstrewn wash. Along the way was a dying rhinoceros beetle on its back with legs feebly waving. I took it out of the hot sun and placed it right-side-up under the shade of an ash tree. If it had to die, I thought, let it be done in comfort.

The August heat, compounded by its humidity, was pressing down on me by the time I stopped for lunch. It was a particularly welcome respite because, praise be, I had a pool in which to plunge. This oasis had formed at the base of a fifty-foot rock-slide and was closed in spectacularly by steep walls of smooth grey granite. In other journals I've written of the near-climactic sensation of being over-heated by the desert sun and drained by hiking under its unrelenting radiance — and then, joy of joys, slipping into the shadowy waters of an ever-cold pool. The glory of it bears repeating! I lingered there for nearly an hour before pushing on campwards.

It was almost three o'clock when I got back. I'd been afoot, on the move, for seven hours. A vigorous day, made all the more enjoyable by being free of that accursed backpack. The day which had dawned with a clear and cloudless sky was now dimmed by thunderheads summoning forces aloft. I spread out the foampad between two ash trees in the sacred grove and hoped for some writing time. But raindrops began to patter on my paper — and, besides, my eyelids were drooping from the day's exertions. So much for the writing. Putting pen to paper outdoors rather than indoors requires so much more discipline. And yet how much more agreeable writing under, say, a canopy of trees and far from the clamour of the noisy animal, the one who cannot stand silence or solitude, *Homo racketus*.

As the thunder growled louder, I darted around the camp, covering the backpack with a plastic sack, stuffing clothes and shoes and everything soakable inside the tent and wondering when, if ever, I'd be able to make a cooking fire for dinner. Just before five o'clock and, after I'd battened down the hatches, the rain started in earnest. The wind blew mightily, the lightning flashed ferociously, the thunder thundered thunderingly, the rain lashed down. And there I was, in my flimsy little tent of blue nylon, without a flysheet, stark naked and feeling vulnerable. For those of us who have trouble with our egos from time to time, an elemental experience such as this can be quite humbling. During a storm, far from all human support systems and quite at the mercy of Mother Nature, there is no room for an inflated ego.

As with most summer storms, its fury was soon spent and, *gracias a Madrecita*, the rain slackened and let me cook up a quick pan of pre-packaged spaghetti and a cup of cocoa. I crouched over this hastily conceived "gourmet dinner" inside the rain-damp tent and hungrily gobbled it up. The tent let in rivulets of rainwater but most of it was absorbed at ground level by the carpet of duff laid down by my friends, the ash trees. So, in spite of more torrents after dark, I stayed dry, all huddled up in my army-issue mummy bag.

Third Day

Rose at six a.m. again. Today I wanted to be back from the morning's side-hike by noon. This would mean limiting myself to two-and-a-half hours out and the same time back. Yesterday had been too strenuous — and there'd been no solid time for writing this journal. At seven a.m. I was off downcreek once more, soon marvelling at a delicate display by small yellow butterflies sipping nectar from tiny blue flowers at the water's edge. And then again at three miniscule mushrooms, cream-coloured, that had found life in a warped dead tree-root. Before long, I had cut away from the creek up to a jumble of yellow-sandstone boulders that gave promise of caves and curious crevices. I was glad to be out of the leafy constraints of the shallow canyon and in rolling open desert again. I was exultant at the solitary unencumbered freedom of it all and sang a song of thanksgiving for having been given the physical ability and the will to be doing what I was doing. To be knowing what I was knowing. I thought of those deep-reaching words of don Juan in Carlos Castañeda's book:

> Para mi solo recorrer los caminos que tienen corazón, cualquier camino que tenga corazón. Por ahi yo recorro y la única prueba que vale es atravesar todo su largo. Y por ahi, yo recorro, mirando, mirando, sin aliento. (For me there is only the travelling on paths which have heart, whatever path that may have heart. There I travel and the only worthwhile challenge is to walk its whole length. And there I wander, looking, looking, breathlessly.)

On this day, I rejoiced in the sure knowledge of being on a path with heart. But even paths with heart have catclaw bushes to contend with and soon found myself in the thick of them. Those catclaw acacias rip the clothes and lacerate the flesh — and the only safe way I know through a patch of them is to step high and then firmly down on the curved-thorn branches. Then they yield but do not break, allowing passage. Yet, if one persists in wearing shorts (as I do), one risks being bloodied on the arms and legs during a roam in the outback. Never worry, they're honourable wounds — those bestowed by the desert.

Today's desert rovings took me up a now-and-then-watered gulch that led to a tight valley finely flanked by junipered slopes and a regal red-rock escarpment. Came upon a weathered Mexican corral of cribbed posts and an old ram-shackle feed-barn rotting away in the desert sun. The rancher's reach into these wildlands is a long one, to be sure. Trying to work around the thickets of scratchy scrub oak, I wound my way upwards out of this peaceful valley, topped the high ridge, and started down the other side. I moved easily for a while, skirting the upper slope but then, dropping too low, became entangled in a boggy, bushy gully. Before getting clear of this thicket, I bashed and bloodied my left shin. No bones broken, though — and that's the biggest blessing of any mishap on a lonely trek like this. In fact, I made it back in one piece minutes before midday, right on schedule. The very first act of homecoming was to drop the shorts, kick off the tennies and slide into that precious pool — with the usual rhapsodic "Aaaagh!" The blood and dust and sweat were washed off in a trice and I rose out of that holy water as pure as a baptismal babe.

Lunch over with, I set up the foam pad in the favoured spot and wrote up this journal for a full four hours. It was something I had to do then and there on a day-by-day basis, because experience had shown that I didn't have the will to do it, from notes, once back at the cabin. Out of nine solo treks (from 1978 to 1987 — last year, 1986, I missed owing to my five months' sojourn in England), I had put together seven journals, including this one. Though there were ominous rumblings in the distance, the afternoon stayed balmy and bright. At five p.m. it was real relief to set aside the paper and put down the pen — the strain of concentration upon mind and eyes, while writing intensely, was always a considerable one.

After supper, I wandered up the creek a ways and came to the slender stately primroses. One bud, its curled yellow petal already showing thro' the green casing that held it, was ready to open — and, privy to this primrose's habit of crepuscular blooming, I was bent on being there for the grand opening. Thus, full of great expectations, I stood over the bud, watching it intently and waiting. And waiting. Nothing happened. I had been there for fifteen minutes and my Anglo-Saxon impatience was beginning to needle me. Twilight — and all of a sudden the thin cigar-shaped bud quavered and started to swell. One green holding sliver was flung downwards, as if sprung, and — marvellous to behold — the tightly-wrapped-around petal unfolded within a few seconds and became a new-born flower. I stood in awe.

A friend recently wrote this to me:

> I hope you enjoy your journeys this summer. You have seen and appreciated what few men will have seen when they have lived out their days. How few of us appreciate what God has given us to wonder at and enjoy.

His words moved me.

Night fell. As I slipped into the tent and lay me down to sleep, the call of the screech owl and the poor-will floated mournfully through the freshly-gathered darkness.

Fourth Day

Daybreak, marked by the first birdcall, was five a.m. I was up thirty minutes after that, and on the trail before the hour was out. Instead of following the creek-bed (now quite familiar) I tried for a shortcut, heading behind camp up the long gradual incline and slipping down the other side of the saddle to where there was a rutted jeep track. Old Sol was gilding the mountain tops by the time the saddle was reached and so, according to daily ritual, I turned and saluted him with a "*¡Buenos dias!*" The Welsh poet W. H. Davies echoed my solar sentiments so fondly when he wrote

> Good morning, Sun, and all things glad and beautiful!
> My pockets nothing hold
> But he who holds the gold,
> The Sun, is my great friend;
> His spending never ends.

In an hour, I had made the old road and unlike the random rovings of the first few days, my course was fixed for me. I wanted to find out where it led and to savour the terrain it wandered through. And wander it I did, turning and twisting —along canyonsides, around cliffs and buttes and even through mountain vales. This was high and dry land. Such water as there was, muddy and unappetising, had been artificially trapped in stock ponds. Had I been desperate, I would've drunk it — but, anticipating a waterless walk, was carrying a gallon and more in my canteen and knapsack. There were no cattle at the stock ponds, thankfully, but neither were there any deer or large wildlife. Only a jackrabbit and a cottontail now and then.

At one point, a glint on glass beneath a bush caught my eye and, checking more closely, I fished out a vintage bottle with its metal cap rust-sealed on it. It was of elegant shape, in perfect condition and embossed with a crest and the words LOS ANGELES PHARMACAL CO. LOS ANGELES, CAL. On the bottom was a trademark, the figure 2, and the date, 1956. It had lain under that isolated bush for thirty-one years, I imagined, and had defied all weathers. I couldn't help wondering whether Los Angeles Pharmacal Co. were still in business.

Further along the route was another treat in store for me, a sun-bleached deer skull and antlers, quite complete. I decided to lug it back and make a present of it to Brian and Holly Richter, managers of the Arizona Nature Conservancy's Hassayampa Preserve in Wickenburg. Naturalist friend Jeffrey Cooper and I had already kicked off their skull collection with a wicked-horned cow and a sharp-tusked javelina, both desert finds.

The heartening thing about this track I was exploring was that it had not been walked or ridden on for a long while. There were no tyre marks and much vegetation had crept back to heal it. Nothing gladdened me more than to see wildland unmarked by man and his confounded machines. It had not escaped the blight of beer cans, however, so as I tramped along I picked them up from the verges and tossed them into midroad for collection upon the return journey. It was not, for the most part, new trash. Some of the cans had been thrown by the beerbarians years ago. But, being aluminum, it was going nowhere for centuries to come. The remoter the land, the greater the proportion of bottles and cans in overall litter. On this stretch, I estimated ninety-five per cent. It angered me to realize that, if the bottle bill (mandatory deposit legislation) had not been outvoted (sixty-eight to thirty-two per cent) on the citizens' referendum in November 1982, this state of Arizona would by now be rid of the bane of bottle and can litter. Those who believed the brainless bullshit concocted by the beverage industry against the bottle bill — and voted No on it — should hang their heads in shame.

The jeep trail finally attained the flat top of a mesa and brought me to an elevation of well over 5,000 feet. The vegetation had altered dramatically. On these wind-raked heights, it had grown sparse, with the hardy and huge alligator-junipers holding sway. Their unusual name comes from the squared and scaled bark, mocking the hide of the great reptile. Interspersed with the alligators were coarse clumps of the wiry beargrass, used for basket-weaving by the Native Americans, and the odd oak tree. The Spanish word *mesa* means *table* in English — and mesas are indeed nature's tabletops that can stretch for miles in their outlandish evenness, flung fortress-like above the rest of the natural world. Made by volcanoes that spill their erosion-resistant and runny magma in a pool instead of through a cone. Take the trees away from these strongholds of solitude, plant them with heather and bracken and gorse — why! they could be the moorlands of Yorkshire, more so on a mist-filled day. Shades of my native heath, indeed.

On the northernmost downslope of this mesa, I stretched out under the branches of a juniper and ate the lunch I'd packed. I had been on foot for five hours, double my intention. The sun was high — and the time had come to turn about. Because of fatigue and mounting heat, the known way home had lost much of its original magic. The sweeping vistas of the tremendous and illimitable terrain below began to pall. The eyes, earlier eager and uplifted, lowered to watch the endless ground beneath the feet. The walk became a trudge — and all I could think of was the closest place that could be called home, a clearing beside a grove of ash trees, a frail small tent of blue, and a cool, cool pool.

I plodded along for hours, for miles — and once in a while Old Sol would dodge behind a billowing cloud, hide his burning brilliance, and send me the great gift of shade. Weary as I was by mid-afternoon, I was stubborn enough not to abandon the task of picking up those bloody beer cans that had been set out along the wending way. Perversely, I began to count them: one, two, three — stoop — twenty- five, twenty-six, twenty-seven — stoop — eighty-eight, eighty-nine, ninety — stoop.... By three o'clock, when about to cut off crosscountry, I had reached a count of 125 cans. The garbage sack was bulging and burdensome. I tied it up, set it visibly in the middle of the narrow road, and dragged dead branches in barrier fashion behind it. It was my hope, quite simply, that the driver of the next jeep or pickup on the scene would have the decency to take this sack back home with him. Of one thing I made sure — he would have to stop and, at the very least, handle the sack in order to be able to pass on his way.

I was back in camp by four p.m., having been out and about for ten hours. That blesséd pool again claimed my body in water worship. Climactic cries rang through the quiet of the canyon!

There remained no reserve of strength for writing or even reading. I just pottered around the campsite, wanting nothing more than repose and relaxation. After cooking up the usual mush of rice and vienna weenies, I took a pillow, a pocketwatch, and paperback (Thoreau's *Walden*, no less), and strolled, stark naked, up the creek to the place of the primroses. This time I was organized for petal peering as a proper Anglo-Saxon should have been.

It was about seven o'clock when I hunkered down on a log, positioned for the evening's grand opening. My impatience problem had been eased by the worthy company of Thoreau himself. There were three suitably swollen, yellow-tipped buds on the point of unfolding. Between readings, I focused on the one nearest to me. Lo and behold! at 7:15 p.m. the expanding primula bud, making its dusk début, was transformed into a precious petal before my very eyes. Within less than a minute, the two other beauteous blooms unfurled. And it was not long before a fat-bodied brown moth, busily buzzing, had alighted on all three fresh-born flowers and, seeking nectar, burrowed its proboscis into their depths. These marauding moths made several penetrations and, pollinating as they went, gave meaning to these fragile flowers that would live for but a night. As a salutation to their brief beingness and in humble thanksgiving, I touched them lightly with my lips before the darkness closed around me.

In the wee small hours I awoke to the sound of rustling in the leaves outside the tent. Curious to know my nocturnal visitor, I shone a flashlight through the screen. It was a skunk grubbing for insects at the base of the ash trees.

"Hóla, Zorra," I said sleepily.

Fifth Day

The clouds hung heavy in the sky this morning. The air was fresh with the promise of rain. With the cut-out plastic gallon jug serving as a portable wash-basin, I went thro' the early morning washing and shaving ritual, squatting on a smooth rock at the streamside. It is said that an Englishman, in addition to going out in the midday sun with mad dogs, will also, in the desert, use the last of his water to shave with. Since I do shave every day, even when alone on a desert trek, I must admit to still fitting that stereotype.

Undeterred by the overcast sky, I was off and hiking by six a.m. I kept to the creekbed for a half-hour or so and then branched off up a tributary arroyo. The morning light faded, rain began to fall, softly at first and then with growing force. Instinctively I took shelter beneath an overhang in the streambank but, minutes later, chose not to crouch there staying dry but to get out into the rain — and give myself over to the experience of walking in it. I was drenched in seconds but mentally freed from the worry and discomfort of it. Because it was summer, there was no real chill to it — and I would dry off quickly enough. With conscious choice and a willingness to do it, it suddenly felt quite fine to be rock-hopping along a gulch with the rain streaming down my face and soaking me to the skin. It was the sort of thing that John Muir, in his quest for the elemental in Nature, loved to do. True, his friends called him Crazy John, but there was likely a tinge of envy in that affectionate name-calling. Old John of the Sierras, so much a spiritual inspiration to me, spoke for me when he wrote

> I will follow my instincts, be myself for good or ill — and see what will be the upshot. As long as I live, I'll hear waterfalls — and birds and winds sing. I'll interpret the rocks, learn the language of flood, storm, and the avalanche. I'll acquaint myself with the glaciers and wild gardens ... and get as near the heart of the world as I can.

I know just what Muir means.

This rain was not long in stopping — but how rich and fecund the earth smelt after its refreshment. Gary Nabhan, a friend of the Sonoran if ever there was one, wrote a lovely book called *The Desert Smells Like Rain*. That title sang tenderly in my mind as I walked on in the sunshine that had so swiftly ousted the rain. What a sweet celebration the summer rains must be for the desert plants and animals parched by the seasonal drought of May, June, and half of July. What joy to know an end to the long dusty deprivation.

Leaving the tight environs of the gulch buried between two ranges, I took an unused and overgrown road upwards into the openness and light. This ended abruptly in a packtrail, long lost but still marked with rock cairns here and there, and it in turn led me over a high rise and down into a grassy watershed. Above that towered a series of redrock ramparts. A defile through these battlements brought me to another valley of sorts. Here in the middle of nowhere was an abandoned cabin, dilapidated, dirty, and forlorn. The tin roof was riddled with holes. I supposed the next wild windstorm would remove what was left of it. The interior was sordid but, in spite of that, it was clear that some deserteers had had the stomach to spend the night there. There were three scribblings on a note pinned to the wall by a rusty nail. They read as follows:

> Welcome to Survival #5 Cabin. Arrived Sat. evening in the midst of a rainstorm. There are four of us young survivalists who are on a 21 day trek thru the Sonoran Desert. It is day 6 for us. [Dated February 15th — 1987, I presumed.]
>
> This trip I thougt would be realy stupid and coming to this cabin makes me more homesick but we got out of the rainstorm truthfuly. I hope I never see this cabin again! [sic] [I hoped they never did, too.]
>
> Thanks. It wasn't much of a cabin but I could see it used to be a nice place. I was glad for a roof over my head. [This one was signed with a feather — a bit unnerving because that was my own personal trademark.]

Possessive of all desert places that I'd worked hard to find, I felt irritated that others had chanced upon this secluded spot — and not so many months ago. Well, at least they hadn't vandalized what remained of the hut.

I never fail to marvel how bone-dry arroyos in the desert can turn into living streams — and the other way round. This dryness is commonly found at the wider end of the arroyo where the land levels out. Often roads cross the dry portion — which is a godsend because, were there flowing water, every weekend warrior and his woman would make a stop there and help destroy the area. It is for the adventuresome to discover the desert oases further back in the cleft of the hills. On this particular day, by dint of some serious hiking, I found my oasis and spent some carefree moments splashing there like a child. Not without cost, though, for one time my sneakers, slick from wading, did not grip fast on a big boulder — and I ended up bouncing down on it on my belly and skinning flesh from knuckles. A bit of fat in the belly parts cushioned the blow.

One friend I had yet to meet up with on this trek was Old Crotalus, the rattlesnake. No solo was ever complete without that meeting. These thoughts were much in my mind as I was avoiding a bottle-neck in the creekbed by scrambling partway up the brushy cliff. Sure enough, like a dream answered, there within two feet of my descending left foot (by then frozen into immobility) lay an Arizona black rattlesnake. He was calmly sunning himself and at first oblivious to my looming over him. The diamond markings were discernible but subdued, being black on a charcoal body; the ivory-white rattle had six or seven segments which declared an age well into maturity. Like most Arizona blacks (often misnamed timber rattlers), he was a serene sort and made no move to coil or rattle. When I gingerly withdrew my foot a couple of feet, he became aware of my invasion, turned tail, and swiftly sought the safety of the undergrowth in the lithest of flights. Guessed his length at about three-and-a-half feet. I shall say it again. The rattlesnakes I have come upon — and there have been many — have, bar none, been of a benevolent disposition. Once in a while they've come close enough to strike at me, yet never have they done so. Earlier this summer, out of sheer instinctual fright, I did a silly aerial dance right above a rattlesnake at rest — and it never moved a muscle. Afterwards, I felt foolish and apologized to it. My ever amicable encounters with rattlesnakes in the wild have led me to vigorously defend their right to be left in peace.

Today's walkabout was also a ten-hour one — longer than planned since, on the return trip, I missed a turning to the trailhead and had no choice but to take the lengthier route by way of a dust-dry watercourse. When the canteen gets low and starts to rattle a bit and the sun hammers down without letting up, a sense of apprehension builds — and the hike rapidly loses its lightness of heart, becoming a resolute and measured march. Sobering is the knowledge that one misstep — with a resulting twisted ankle or broken leg — could bring on a drawn-out death within days. Yes, it was good to reach water again.

Spent the late afternoon resting up and absorbing the divine quiet of the natural world about me. The varied birdsong was pleasing. I resumed my vocal exchange with the crested silky black flycatcher (phainopepla) whose single piping note always from the same locale told me he was a habitué of these parts and, like Thoreau, did not care to wander too far from his home. Even that odd muted puppy-whine of the roadrunner filtered thro' the trees from the desert slopes above me.

Sixth Day

Saturday already. This particular one was my sabbath, in the Jewish tradition. A day of rest at least from foot-journeying, if not from journal-writing. The latter had fallen behind so a blitz on it was called for. I was gratified at having got into the spirit of this journal because at the outset of the trek had felt sluggish about it. After ablutions and coffee this morning, I propped myself up between the two tall trunks and started penning at 6:40 a.m. It was noon before I put down pen and broke for lunch. At 1:10 p.m., began again; I had nearly put in the equivalent of a full day at the office — with just fourteen pages to show for it. Ah, well, I had played all week. Now I had to work.

I could scarcely believe that the week was virtually over, that tomorrow I'd be heading homewards. The time had sped by at a pace that seemed even unfair. I should not have had to pack up and leave so soon — I'd only just got there, damn it! Perhaps next year's solo, the tenth, could be extended to ten days — though if that were so, I'd need a helicopter to ferry in the food for that long. Perish the thought. I know that it is trite to say that time flies — because everybody is only too conscious of that inescapable fact. The fact that time, if you believe in it, does fly makes me all the more aware of the compelling need to live life fully and vividly in the here and now, to make the present moment count. And in order to be able to do that, I must pare away all that is trivial and inessential to me. Thoreau said it succinctly:

> I wanted to live deep and suck out all the marrow of life ... to live so sturdily and Spartan-like as to put to rout all that was not life....

It occurred to me on one of my desert wanderings that our English language had no noun or adjective or verb or adverb to describe and celebrate this vital and sacred charge to live in the Eternal Now (as some philosophers have called it). The reason for this is simple. Culturally and spiritually, the last thing we have been taught is to revere the present moment. We are, however, skillful at the dubious arts of living stuck in the past or of being in love with the future. Anyway, undaunted by this lamentable lack of the right terms, I coined them.

Nowness is the state or condition of being in the now. *Nowfulness* is the ability to live wholly in the now. *Nowlessness* is the inability to do that. To be *nowful* is the intransitive verb (not dissimilar from to be joyful, I might add) and *nowlessly* and *nowfully* are the respective adverbs. What could be more delightful than getting a letter from another human being signed, "Yours Nowfully"?

Today turned into a scriptural marathon. I wrote for eight-and-one-half hours and couldn't remember the last time there was such an outpouring from this pen. One of English literature's most prolific writers, D. H. Lawrence, used to strive to balance his feverish writing episodes with a spell of plain manual labour, such as chopping wood. I myself was not as energetic as that, preferring simply to saunter along the creek and in that fashion to unwind from the day's intellectual effort. After making the same old supper and using the daylight left to prepare as best as could be for a daybreak departure, I went back to the creekside, perched on a boulder, and let darkness envelop me. The fireflies, ever faithful in their nightly performance, were there again. This time I perceived that it was a greenish light given off by these phosphorescent phantoms of the twilight. Tonight, though, they were dramatically upstaged by a lambent light appearing on the eastern horizon. It was the rising of an all but full moon. I watched with wonder.

Much rustling and carrying on in the brush on the bank behind me put me on the alert for a night-roaming skunk. Feeling a bit vulnerable in my nocturnal nudity, I stayed still and picked up a long thin branch — for skunk discouragement, if need be. This white-backed, snowy-tailed animal shambled straight towards where I sat — and didn't halt when he should have. Startled, I shot up from the rock — and up shot his bushy tail, ready for action. He appeared to make a pass at me, so I held the stick at arm's length and pointed straight at him. Was it to be fight or flight? Fortunately for me, he opted for the latter and shuffled off into the bushes. To have been skinny-sprayed would've been a foul affair. This minor contretemps put an end to my meaningful musings and I retired, without ado, to the screened-in security of the tent in the trees.

Just before fading into sleep, I heard the hooting of the screech owl and from the familiar direction knew it to be the same caller as on all previous nights.

Seventh Day

Nature's early alarm, the first birdsong, had me up at the crack of dawn. It was five a.m. and it took me fifty minutes to pack up, to remove all traces of my occupancy at the campsite and be on the trail. I'd already reconnoitered the way up and out of the canyon — and had even cleared away fallen branches, tangled twigs, and other obstacles. It promised to be a punishing climb out and therefore, to beat the sun and to benefit from the cool of the first hours, an early start was imperative. I struck a lively pace and followed a gully, choked in places with bristly chaparral. As it snaked upwards it broadened and was easier to negotiate. I passed several seeps and small springs; above them had formed a leafy umbrella of great-branched sycamore trees. Time to fill up with water. Where I was bound for, another lofty plateau, would be dry — and I might well be up in that dryness for a day and a night. Not unreluctantly, I chose to carry two full gallons and two halves — at eight pounds per gallon. That made an extra load of twenty-four pounds. Happy for me that I'd eaten down that deadweight of food supplies — otherwise I could not have borne this added burden.

I set off up the steepening gully — and God! was the backpack now a brute. But there was no choice. I had to have that water with me. As the altitude increased so did the boulders in size. With grunts, gasps, and groans (yes, I too had become the noisy animal), I flogged and slogged my way up to the rim of that mesa. It would've been an unthinkable chore under the noonday sun but, even as I cursed and sweated at every upward step, I blessed the shade that made it possible then. There were no less than three rattlesnakes along the path of that arduous ascent. The largest was the first, a western diamondback, I believe. The other two were young with undeveloped rattles and a reddish tinge to their scales — possibly the tiger species. All three of these reptiles were in a state of quiet repose, doubtless relishing the cool of the morning and perhaps even digesting the prior night's catch. Not one of these somnolent snakes reared or rattled at me. The smallest of the trio was curled up on the jutting shelf of a rock that was right in the middle of my passageway. Only feet away from this snake (whose head had bobbed back upon my approach), I had to edge around the rock with infinite gentleness. I wished each a good morning, thanked them for their respectful and kindly conduct — and continued ever upward. *Excelsior!* It was worthy of note that I had never before come across three rattlesnakes in a twenty-four-hour period and certainly not in the space of one hour.

The mesa heights were gained in an hour and fifty minutes. Before moving on, I slaked my thirst, rested awhile, and rearranged the water-load. It was better for me to carry one gallon in the hand and another strapped to the pack than to bear both gallons on my back. Finding a rocky rancher's road, I stayed with its windings and weavings for miles but after what I'd just been through, was perfectly contented with that.

Not much vegetation on this sky-island — a scattering of Utah junipers which sent me their sweet cedar-smell on the wind, a covering of short coarse grass interwoven with the unnumbered millions of lichen-laced stones and rocks flung everywhere, irregular patches of scrub oak, some yucca baccata — bayonet-leafed plants with their pale-green football-fruits dangling from them. No alligator junipers here, though. Why should one mesa have had them and another not? Ah, Madrecita has her many mysteries. Once in a great while, if we are patient and deserving, she will reveal one to us.

And such a revelation is the rarest of gifts.

Eventually, by mid-morning, I came to a place close to where I would make my descent back into the world of human beings — and decided to seek the shade of a gnarled juniper and stay put for the rest of the day, writing and reflecting. I needed to summon up strength and resolve to leave the solitude I wasn't really ready to leave. Levelling off a spot up against the soft-barked trunk of the old juniper, I whiled away the sultry afternoon writing copiously. It was in my mind to spend the night there — in full moonlight on the mesa — but flotillas of sullen grey thunderheads were massing likes ships of war to the north and they appeared hellbent on making my mesa their port of call. Since the rockiness of the land didn't allow even a single tent-space, I elected to make my way down and start homewards after supper. At the point of departure, around 6:30 p.m., sierras both to the north and west were being doused by slanting sheets of summer rain. Before descending from the mesa top, I turned and said a fond farewell, arms upraised toward the sinking sun.

"Sorry, *Zopilote*, not this time," I said to the turkey vulture that floated high above me. "*¡Adios, Cuervos!*" I cried to the six ravens circling in the sky; in reply, they croaked a valediction.

At seven o'clock, down on the dirt road finally, the long and last march began. With a lightened load, I kept up a rhythmic pace and before I knew it the day had gone and the night had come. A couple of cars went speeding by me, weekend stragglers — the first humans I'd laid eyes on for an entire week. No attempt to hitch-hike on my part — I could hardly write about man's infernal machines and then be the first to avail myself of them. Besides, it was somehow important for me to complete the journey on foot. And so I did. It took me all of five hours, a distance of about fourteen miles.

Though the walk had become a march and the march a drudgery, I was privy to special sights of the night. By the roadside there were glow-worms, much like grounded fire-flies, but their luminescence was constant. They had that greenish glow, too. I caught sight of a pair o' poor-wills whirling in the air with their wide gullets scooping up insects in flight. (The poor-will is often heard in the wilds but seldom seen.)

One hour into this tramp, the menacing clouds got serious and with one prodigious thunderclap opened up on me. The old Rodgers & Hammerstein song, "When you walk through a storm, Keep your head up high, And don't be afraid of the dark," flashed into my mind. This counsel was inappropriate for me since I had to keep my head down and watch the ground in front of me for rattlesnakes. Because of the cloud cover, the full moon wasn't doing her job and I couldn't see that far ahead of me. One could well say that the stormy weather had rained on the moon's parade. I did get a brief glimpse of her — but only once — yellow and squelched between two horizontal banks of black cloud. Sheet lightning, bright and white, hurled flashes that one instant lit up the Earth and the next plunged it into darkness again. I plodded on, glad for the rain that cut the mugginess of the August night. The road was utterly deserted. I was alone with my thoughts and the task of walking. The tempo of the body in the rhythm of motion set the backpack creaking and squeaking like the harness of a mule. And in the last leg of the march — which seemed interminable — with shoulders aching abominably, feet more tender with each step, legs tingling with tiredness, and body reeking sourly of sweat, I knew exactly what it felt like to be a Grand Canyon mule on that homestretch up to Bright Angel lodge.

It was just minutes short of midnight when, dog-tired, I stumbled into the cabin. The wander-week was over and I was back home safely. With the last shred of energy, I lit a hurricane lamp and went down to the creek. I slipped into the water and, in that moment of rapture, looked up through the trees to the sky. There, at long last, was the moon, full and unobscured. She was smiling at me.

> The Earth never tires.
> The Earth is rude, silent, incomprehensible at first.... Nature is rude and incomprehensible at first. Be not discouraged, keep on, there are divine things well-envelop'd.... I swear to you there are divine things more beautiful than words can tell.
>
> — Walt Whitman

VIII: Lluvias de Verano: Summer Rains

Sunday July 15 to Sunday July 22 1990

My state of aloneness began with Sioux's departure on foot at seven a.m. Friday a.m. the thirteenth we had driven the two hours to the trailhead, parked *Chiripa* (her Toyota pickup), and burdened with backpacks (mine carrying ten days' worth of food, so heavier than usual), headed off into the heat of the day. The overloaded pack and the high humidity combined with a lack of sleep the night before made the three-and-one-half-hour footjourney a wearisome business. Nonetheless we were jubilant at being out in a sequestered stretch of desert again — and far from crowds. Though we had been passed by some ranchers in an old Jeep heading homewards, we were fairly sure of being the only souls around for many miles.

Which is precisely what we wanted.

Two days later, when we'd said our farewells and exchanged *abrazos* in a sandy wash that would ultimately lead Sioux back to her truck, I cut off on an old trail which used to be a fisherman's road but was now (blessed be) closed to motorized traffic. There was some eco-work to be done — namely the picking up of an unsightly pile of aluminum beer cans under desert bushes just off the track. The old-fashioned ring tabs indicated that the cans had been there for a long time; had they not been fished out of the undergrowth, they'd have been there for a lot longer — being aluminum and unrustable, they could've been there forever and a day. I crushed them underheel for compact carrying. It felt good to return the sanctity of that tiny patch of desert by erasing all traces of man's mindless mess. More work down the way, breaking up an old whiteman's fire circle, an untidiness of ashes, smoke-blackened rocks, food cans, and scraps of foil. The ashes I finger-raked into a small mound, then scooped them up and scattered them to the four winds. To restore the natural wildness of a place, to wipe away the mark of man, is nothing less than a labour of love — and a small way of saying thank you to Madrecita for the endless gifts she bestows on the desert roamer.

One of her gifts today was the powerful beauty of the Sonoran scenery surrounding me — giant cactuses in abundance, some of them still carrying the scarlet *pitahaya* fruit, thickets of teddybear cholla luminous with summer sunlight, pale green palo verdes throwing thin shade on the desert floor, fat red-spined barrel cacti healthy as hell, feathery-leafed mesquites fresh with recent rain, pincushion mini-cacti crowned with pale pink blooms, and desert willows (catalpas) flowering lavender in the flashflood-smoothed arroyos. And all around the panorama of rugged ranges, layered one upon the other and fading into the blue haze of dream-like distances. Best of all, nothing, not a single thing man-made to jar the dramatic desertness, the natural flow of it all. In short, my kind of country.

As I wandered along, with all the time in the world mine, happy, free, even child-like, I thought of John Muir's own form of bliss, roaming at will in the land he so passionately loved and stood up for, the High Sierras in California. What an inspiration John of the Sierras has been to me in his writings and with his life!

At one point I stopped to pick up a *pitahaya* from the low-slung arm of a saguaro — such sweet and special fruit whose ripening marks the start of the new year for the Tohono O'odham (Papago) people in southern Arizona. I wasn't the only one taken with this desert delicacy — a whitewing dove on an upper arm was dipping its bill into the delectable redness of a split fruit and ants were feasting on those that had fallen to the earth. Close by was some scat of Brother Coyote (my totem animal), black with the shiny, tiny seeds of the saguaro. All creatures of the Sonoran love *pitahaya* — and I'm no exception. Little chance of starvation this trip — there were bushes full of sweet, orange hackberries and ripe mesquite beans aplenty. Madrecita is ever provident to those who love her.

Tramping up a narrow curving gully I heard the abrupt rattle of hooves on loose rock above me and caught a fleeting glimpse of mule deer. Yesterday there had been a pair of bolting javelina spotted. A screeching red-tailed hawk high on the wing, persistent in its complaint, told me that a nest with young was nearby, maybe lodged in the prickly crotch of some venerable saguaro. They soar so high in the sky, those redtails, like eagles. What must they think when they spot a ground-bound human plodding along in the sweltering heat below them?

I followed the trail, washed out in places and showing no signs of fresh use (to my delight) until it dropped down from the stony heights and met with the river. Came across a new cattle fence which did not belong in this untrammeled area. The consolation was that I could see no cows anywhere. The trail gate was novel, however; it was weighted by an iron bell and shut itself automatically after being opened. Most of the trail-marking rock cairns were tumbled down — so many years have passed since maintenance has been done on this stretch. The more primitive the better as far as I'm concerned. Refilled my canteen at the river's edge and ambled around the rock-strewn floodplain for a while. Trying to identify a bird with a comical call, I got down on my hands and knees and crawled thro' a stand of bamboo-like carrizo, craning my neck upwards to try to spot the feathered character. But he must've spotted me first and, unimpressed by my all-fours routine, flew off with a zany cackle. Moments later I was startled by the harsh croak of a great blue heron flushed from a dense stand of riverside cattails. As graceful as that big bird of the water may be, graceless is its cry.

The return journey, essentially a backtrack, took an hour and ten minutes, and I was back in camp by high noon, in time for a lunch of rye crispbread, mashed sardines, a green apple from the cabin tree, and lemonade. Neither the lunch nor the dinner menu would vary one iota for the next seven days. Dull but sustaining.

At three p.m. a summer storm with billowing thunderclouds swept down over the river — and the wind and the rain drove me from the old willow in the cove to the dry shelter of the cave above it. I had been writing up this journal and resumed my work up in the cave. Then, as the rain pelted down, I had a wild urge to walk naked in it. No time or circumstance like the present, thought I, flinging off my clothes and stepping out into the storm. It was exhilarating to body and spirit — chiefly because I'd never done it before. Ah, the thrill of a first experience, whatever it may be! I scrambled over rain-slick rocks to another cave in the cliffside, a hundred or so yards away — and stood in its ancient mouth in the buff and buffeted by the wind, feeling (and no doubt looking) curiously Stone Age. Had river-runners been floating by at that memorable moment, they would've had an intriguing entry for their log. This particular cave was full of dried dung which could have been a mountain lion's, but on breaking it open I saw nothing but plant material in it. Had to be javelina, indeed a whole herd of them.

By the time this rude nude dude got back to his own cave, the driving rain had let up and settled into a drizzle. That meant a cold dinner rather than a panful of steaming brown rice — and no hot coffee. Oh, well, in the words of that infamous Mick Jagger song, "You cain't always git what you want." Although I had a tent up, wasn't sure just how waterproof it was, so decided to play safe and sleep in the bone-dry cave. With it facing the east and the rising sun (as a traditional Navajo hogan), I knew I'd be up earlier than if cloistered in the tent. Early stirrings on these solo sojourns make for good and long morning side-hikes.

Darkness fell a little before eight and just before it did a bevy of bats made several semi-circular swoops in and out of the cave, thoughtfully avoiding my head—just! About the same time, an elf-owl just out of its saguaro hole twittered loudly in a mesquite tree beyond the cave mouth. And a firefly flew up from the river flickering its little lamp in the gathering blackness of the desert night. Dry and warm, I'd hoped to sleep soundly — but didn't, damn it. Some invasive insects, ants probably, and certainly one cone-nose bug (because in the morning I saw it skulking off pumped full of my blood) had me scratching like a monkey all night. And to add to this discomfort, bullfrogs in the river reeds kept honking their klaxon-horns at regular intervals until daybreak. Ah! the joys of communing with Ma Nature.

Monday July 16th 1990

Having set aside some kindling in a dry place before the heavens opened yesterday, I was able to fire up a cup of coffee this a.m. That and a grapefruit sufficed for breakfast. By seven a.m. I was off exploring. Walking quietly up a wide soft-sand arroyo, I caught sight of an adult javelina calmly crossing ahead of me — and oblivious of me. I froze — and another javelina went by, also unsuspecting. Their pace was so delicate and dignified, yes, that I stayed still for several more minutes, not wanting to spoil their serenity by the shock of my human presence. This tactic worked. They continued on their wild way undisturbed.

Following washes, at least until they tighten up and become brushy, is a pleasant pastime on desert roamabouts. They don't demand the same effort and caution that, say, a loose talus slope does. One has the luxury of closer observation. I noticed a packrat's nest, fortified with spiny cholla balls, in a crevice in the wall of the wash — an unusual home for Old *Neotoma* who normally prefers flat land with plenty of cactuses. Bright red bits of fluff, insects but smaller than velvet ants, scurried around the sandy floor of the water-course. Here and there an isolated cottonwood, vivid in its light greenness, spread high over the squat mesquites clinging to the arroyo banks. These few "trees of life" did not live up to their name since no pool of springwater glistened around their bases. There were *tinajas*, though — rock hollows filled with rainwater; one of them, oddly, had a dead mouse floating in it.

As I pushed upwards, doing a sort of dance from boulder to boulder and gaining elevation quickly, the canyon deepened and with its steep craggy sides of salmon-coloured rock took on the aspect of a colossal natural cathedral. The south-facing slope was literally forested with strong saguaros so plentiful and precipitously placed that, in the soft light of early morning, the vista seemed surreal. I had never before seen the like of it. Utah junipers, the sure sign of having gained 3,000 feet, were scattered here and there — their dark-green complementing the light of the cottonwoods and saguaros. And that, too, of the ocotillos, which refoliate and defoliate not according to season like most plants but according to rainfall or lack thereof.

Dropping back down, I was struck by the dearth of ripe fruit on the jojoba bushes. This time of year is when the harvest of jojoba nuts is best — and yet there wasn't a single one on any of the many bushes. Strange, but perhaps cyclical.

Taking a shortcut over a hill to reach the main wash leading back to my river-camp, I stumbled upon an Indian ruin with the tell-tale potsherds littered about the tumbled down walls. I wondered where the nearest spring was all those centuries ago — or had the native peoples trudged the mile or so to the river for their water? Found a distinctive piece of pottery that was part of the bottom of a jug and then had to fight the possessive need to take it away with me. My better instincts won the day. I put it back on the ground. The hill was thick with giant cactuses — how the ancient ones must've feasted in *pitahaya* season!

Eleven o'clock saw me back at the cove. This well-tried pattern, during summer solos, of exercise and explorations in the morning and reading, writing, or ruminating in the afternoon, continues satisfactorily for me. It makes a nice balance and rounds out the day. After last night's sleeplessness, I decided to quit the cave of the cone-nose and move the tent away from the riverside — out of earshot of the bellowing bullfrogs. I set it up again, this time on a flat dirt patch around the bend in the wash, but out of the flood path. This proved to be a wise move because, true to form for July, thunderclouds assembled armylike in the late afternoon. To the angry accompaniment of crashing thunder and fierce forked lightning, the wildest of storms hit. This one had me cowering in the cave, with not the slighest impulse to flounce around starkers in the rain again. It came down in buckets, hard and unyielding for half an hour. A full inch must've fallen in that short time. At the front of the cave a rivulet began to flow but in the back I kept dry. This was a terrific tempest — and I had a grandstand view of it. All of a sudden the river started to muddy up — and with a roar of prodigious power a raging flood in the cove creek tore into the mainstream. This roiling, boiling deluge from upcreek — a classic desert flashflood — had me open-mouthed in wonder. And it also had me worried. Some of my gear, not the least being the backpack and all supplies, still sat on the grassy river bank. It was in jeopardy.

In the thick of this mad maelstrom, I left the safety of the cave, shinned down the cliff and, with a wary eye on the furious flood (which was cresting the creeksides), frantically dragged everything to higher ground. I was only out in a few minutes, but it was one drenched and bedraggled desert rat who hauled himself back into that blessed cave. Before long, the squall had lurched off into the west and all grew calm again. So short yet so sharp. I was amazed and amused to see a flotilla of ten ducks pass by, bobbing madly up and down in the turbulent water, yet, it seemed, quite quackingly happy with it all. Desert flashfloods are a true phenomenon, always captivating to me.

Within two hours of its onset, this particular flood — which at its full spate no power on earth could've resisted — was reduced to a tiny trickle. Someone coming on the scene afterwards would've hardly known that this hellion had happened. Oh, Madrecita, your mysteries are manifold, yea, marvellous.

The sodden state of everything meant another cold and unexciting meal of crisp bread and anæmic vienna sausages. And again no cup of java, one of my last remaining vices. But I had weathered the storm and so had the pup tent. At dusk I carried over my bedding in the hopes of a decent night's sleep. Before night came on, I wandered up the wash which just a few hours before had borne such a tremendous torrent, and even regretted trampling on the finely water-sculpted sand. Nature's consummate artistry — sometimes so ephemeral as with sand — shows itself in many and wondrous forms. And her final showing of the fast-fading day was a Spanish galleon of a black cloud brushed with the blood of the dying sun.

"Buenas noches, Sol," I said. *"Gracias por la vida."* ("Good night, Sun. Thank you for life.")

Tuesday July 17th 1990

I slept quite well and was astir by 6:15 a.m. Washed and shaved in the still chocolate-coloured river which was running high and in haste. In a backwater where flotsam and foam had collected, big fish (possibly bass or carp) were scooping up the surface stuff with round pouting mouths. A curious sight, these foamaphilic fish. Kissable carp, indeed.

It was a sublime morning — not a cloud in the sky and Old

Sol back to luminous life again. The last few days had been cloudy and somehow morose — making me a bit melancholy — so I was cheered by the brilliance of this new day.

Because I was falling behind some on this journal and on camp chores, I chose to make the morning hike a shorter one. I set out to climb the ship-shaped mesa just to the south of the campsite. God, it was a lovely day. And how free I felt. There's such a sense of innocence regained on these solos. For a brief time, seven short days (yet longer than most will ever know, sadly) I am without constraint, am absolutely my own master — with no responsibility to anyone save myself. Actually the latter responsibility is quite a critical one since being without "support systems" I must take the best care of myself. A question of survival, really. Since I have a fundamental faith in the natural world, I don't give in to the "what if ... ? what if ... ?" fears suggested by others and sometimes by my own subconscious — but I don't act recklessly when alone in Nature. I value Life too much to want to play the fool in remote places. So I try to walk gently, to watch closely, and to move in reverence. So far, so good.

And what of the innocence? It is a getting the child back through simply having, making time to commune with Nature — and within that experience, which calls more for days than hours, doing everything possible with mind, body, and spirit to live vividly in the here and now. And one can only hope and pray that a bit of this blessedness, truly a state of grace in a world crazily enamored of the future, can be brought back and carried over into one's everyday life. I agree with the poet and visionary William Blake that beyond the bitterness and disillusionment of worldly experience can lie a new and greater innocence than that of childhood — new and greater because it has been tempered in the fire of life. And that should be our noblest aspiration because it offers the highest reward.

Weaving thro' mesquite bosques and moving steadily up

the alluvial fan at the base of the mesa, I made it to the top without strain and in good time. On the way up the rain-damp slope, I passed through a sun-resplendent stand of teddybear chollas and somehow kicked up a spiny ball into my right calf. Cursing and gritting teeth, I pulled the imbedded needles loose with a comb, an old desert trick. It stung like the devil — some pinpricks of blood but no great harm done.

The strong sunshine had stirred the cicadas into song — every palo verde appeared to have one in it. The morning air, clear as crystal after the rain, vibrated with their tinny shrilling. Singly, when startled out of their perches, they can sound like the first buzz of a rattlesnake — and they're not the only ones startled, believe me.

Tops of mesas are distinctly their own world, in vegetation, aspect, and just plain feel. The panorama encompassing this sky-island was magnificent. Below, the brown river, edged with green, snaking through canyons silent, stern, and unimaginably old. Beyond it, vast and dramatic reaches of Sonoran desert, unique on the face of the Earth. I sat and stared, in a sort of rapture, and said softly, "What a gift of glory this is. What an incredibly lucky man I am."

Poking around this treeless little plateau, I was surprised to find fragments of buff pottery, indicating long ago settlement. But why here so windswept and waterless? Perhaps as a mountain stronghold, the ultimate natural fortress, or maybe simply a lookout? Questions to be ever asked but never answered. There was an abundance of prickly pear on these heights (wuthering in winter, I'm sure). The fruit on them was purple-ripe, so I picked half a dozen *tunas* to liven up my dull diet. Going organic as it were. Because I was, as ethnobotanist Gary Nabhan calls it, gathering the desert, I took some pencil cholla fruit for good measure. All cactus fruit is edible, tho' not necessarily palatable.

Took one last sweeping look at the natural grandeur spread out below and around me as if to fix it forever in my mind's eye, and then began wending my way down the thickly-vegetated *bajada*. I was back at base by ten a.m., giving me a couple of hours before lunch to wax my hiking boots, to flatten and bag a pile of aluminum cans, and to bury the non-recyclable litter I'd picked up. The latter, including beer bottles, was too heavy to pack out, unfortunately.

More of this journalwriting in the afternoon. Yet another storm blustered through in mid-afternoon. Again I was sent scurrying to the cave, clutching foampad, paper and pen. A most violent thunderclap rent the air directly overhead. The very walls of the cave seemed to shudder and I let out an involuntary yelp. Forty-five minutes after the rains came, the second flashflood in two days disgorged itself into the river with much sound and fury. Yet one hour later there was scarcely a trace of it. There must have been a cloudburst upriver, too, because the water in the main channel turned to dark and dirty brown. Not good to bathe in anymore and certainly not to drink.

One of the chief blessings of the campsite is the small but sufficient spring fifty yards back from the creek's confluence with the river. Without its clear, cool water, I'd have to be drinking a mud and weed beverage. Above the spring was a shady canopy of willow trees in which quite a few whitewing doves nested. They were nervous birds, poor things, and flew off with a snap and whir of wings each time I went there for a drink. No peace even for the innocent, it seems.

This evening Madrecita was considerate of my dinner schedule and called quits on the rain in time for me to make an Indian fire and boil up a panful of rice. Even in summer, I enjoy cooking an evening meal when camping out. Some friends cheerfully snack their way thro' an entire backback. Not I. I have a set menu, however boring. Somehow the making of a little fire is a needed ritual for me. *Chacun a son goût*. Each to his own.

Before slipping into the tent at nightfall, I strolled up the wide wash and then veered off up a narrow one. I was flanked on both sides by the living desert. Stopping and listening in the twilight, I heard nothing but quiet and silence.

The desert was at peace and so was I.

Wednesday July 18th 1990

The cheeky strident whistle of a curve-billed thrasher fetched me out of sleep at first light. I needed to be up early, tho'. I had an ambitious exploration in mind for the morning. As I was making coffee, the sun — all a-dazzle — cleared the rim of the great mesa to the east. Each sunrise seems so triumphant, a daily and radiant affirmation of the life-force. And I saluted Old Sol in the spirit of that thought.

Today I had to cross the river, still murky, mucky, and swift of current. The first attempt failed. I got part way across but baulked at the powerful push of the water and the waist-depth of it. Barefoot, I didn't have a strong grip on the bottom so I inched back to dry land. Went upstream a hundred yards and found a shallower place to ford. This time I used a stout stick which helped to shore me up against the down current. Made it, with a cheer, to the other side. I'm not a strong swimmer so water is my Achilles' heel. That'd be true irony — drowning on a desert solo. Once across, I followed the dry upper level of the riverbed, dodging now and then thro' thickets of burro brush till I came to a gulch that led up to a hog's back ridge which separated the river as it made an enormous oxbow bend.

Here, remarkably, the river almost doubled back on itself. I walked the knife-edge of the high ridge and descended by a faint trail to the brushy riverbank, keeping to it till I came to where a canyon debouched into the mainstream. I'd arrived safely where I wanted to be and swung up the canyon away from the river. It was dry as dust to begin with but before long I heard that sweetest of desert sounds — the tinkling trickle of water. It was a perennial flow, too. There were fish in the deeper pools formed where the canyon narrowed. The hiking was slow. There were stretches tangled with carrizo (cane brake), clumps of long-grass, vine creepers, and cattails.

At one point where the cliff walls hemmed in the creek, I had to wade through belly-deep; with the overhanging foliage tangled and lush, I felt as if I were on a jungle expedition in Southeast Asia. And yet some way above me I could make out the saguaros, those sentinels of the Sonoran. A little farther on I came upon a magic place, a fairy grotto with curved, lime-streaked walls of stone down which hung maidenhair fern and velvet mosses. Dripping water from a seep on the cliff had created this hanging garden. A lone, gnarled sycamore rose from the middle of the grotto, its flood-bared roots encircling a pellucid pool in which fishes darted to and fro. Slender bulrushes in one nook and in another *Lobelia cardinalis*, the scarlet cardinal flower of summer, seen only along desert streamsides. This enchanted place, cool and secretive, was soft lit by filtered sunshine from the searing sky above. I lingered there for a while before moving on.

By and by, the canyon opened up and evened out to where the desert was in full view and accessible. I was close to turning around and heading back when I saw it, glinting a stone's throw away. A perfect pool, captured in a smooth granite basin, six or seven feet deep, twenty feet long and the same in width. An emerald gem, as pure as a poem — and simply crying out to be swum in! I flung off my clothes and flung myself in. Bliss. This morning's excursion had ended in serendipity.

Coming out of the canyon to rejoin the river, I happened upon an old and rusting — but still serviceable — spade. What on earth was it doing there? I looked around for evidence of bygone mine workings — but there was nothing of that sort. *¿Quien sabe?* as my Mexican friends would say with a shrug.

The river had not risen (it had been fluctuating day in, day out) since early morning; so, luckily, with my worthy staff working for me, I had no trouble in getting back over to my side.

The customary cumulus cloud build up half way thro' the afternoon — but nothing ominous, meaning a rain-free evening and a full rice bowl. After supper, another eco-chore. In the next arroyo upstream from me, some beerbarians (an Arizona species of the barbarian or *Slobus americanus*) had left a disgusting sackful of camping litter — and I determined to get rid of it as best I could. The tin cans, already oxidizing, I tossed deep into the bushes; the paper, plastics, and styrofoam I burned in a bonfire mid-wash so the next flood would sweep the ashes away; and the thirty-six aluminum cans I hand-crushed with a rock — for lugging out to civilization. The bottles I buried in a sandpit; since they're made of sand, they'll one day return to it, in a million years, they say. I also broke up and dispersed another whiteman's fire-ring, which completed the restoring of the vicinity to its natural, unblemished state. By the time I left, the whole area would be impeccable, Nature's dominion reasserted.

The saunter up the wash at last light, which has become a little ritual in itself, revealed an elf owl — delightful wee creature — perched in the branches of a leafless mesquite. I crept quite near to it as it sat there twittering vocally — but then flew off on its night-time business. A loud humming of bees drew me to a rocky cleft above the border of the wash — obviously a hive tucked away in there, but it was too dark by then to pinpoint it.

Thankful for another day of desert splendour, I went to the tent and slept a solid sleep.

Thursday July 19th 1990

I had a visitor first thing. A jackrabbit, long ears waving like antennae, hopped down from the cove's grassy bank onto the sandbar and took a drink from Big Muddy. It kept an eye on me, but I didn't move a muscle. After nosing around on the wet sand, it gave a couple of rear-leg skips and vanished as quickly as it had come. Cottontail rabbits I've come across this trip, but no jackos till now. Brilliant blue-sky day today.

One more big wash to explore. Way up it there's a distant just-visible cottonwood tree which gives the promise of springwater. Within minutes of setting off, a coyote chorus struck up, one pack answering another. It's the call of not only the wild but of pure freedom to me and never fails to thrill me to the marrow. Of all the animals that roam the Sonoran desert, it is with the coyote that my spirit identifies most fondly. God's dog, the Native Americans call him. To me he's *hermanito,* little brother.

Passed thro' a colony of saguaros, one or two with ripe and reachable fruit on their armtips, so I breakfasted on fresh *pitahaya.* Delicious! *¡Sabroso!* This is the quintessence of quail country. Coveys of these feathered footsoldiers under every other bush, clucking and cooing, pecking and wooing. Not wanting to disturb one covey ahead of me, I took a detour and let them be. No danger from this walking-upright stranger. While it is true that I have reverence for life-forms other than human, I am not as considerate to them as I might be. There's been some effort made in this direction, tho'. Where spider webs are strung across trails, I try to go around rather than through them; if for some reason I lift up a rock and there's life — such as an ants' nest — beneath it, I'll put the rock back and use another. Imagine having the roof of your home torn off in the heat of summer. If I unwittingly step on a plant, I'll straighten it out and prop it up, if need be. If I'm throwing out dishwater, I'll aim it towards a bush that looks thirsty. This is what Aldo Leopold in his *Sand County Almanac* called an "extension of ethics." By that he meant an ethical dimension beyond the responsibility of human to human. It's actually a minute-by-minute discipline which gradually brings with it a new and heightened awareness (and respect) for all life. There's a bit of joy in there, too. Never mind that people may think you strange. They have their own oddities, God knows!

Spotted a beer can wedged beneath a fat prickly pear. As I fell on all fours to yank it free I saw the egg cocoon of a black widow spider dangling in her untidy web close to the can. No sign of the widow herself, so I gingerly reached in my hand and quick as lightning did what I had to do. Apologized to the lady in black and red for my inconsideration in disturbing her spiderly space and went on my way, shaking dirt out of the can — rather carefully.

As it gained height, the wash was eventually pinched in to a tight gully. Junipers began to appear. I seemed to have arrived at an altitude level with that of the top of the mesa I'd climbed two days before. (I could see it in the far and hazy distance.) At one point I was entranced to be able to look down on the dark brown shining back feathers of a turkey vulture as it soared on the thermal currents of air high above the earth but below me. Its wrinkled red neck and bald head were constantly flicking from side to side watching out for the carrion that would make up its next macabre meal. "*¡Hola, Zopilote!*" I shouted good-naturedly into the wind. Tho' I wished this big bird of death well, the wish was not at my own expense.

I did attain the goal of the morning, that lone cottonwood. This time it lived up to its tree-of-life reputation. A trickle of water ran by it, but the water looked only temporary. Cottonwoods will not survive without lots of moisture. Interestingly, when they've drunk their fill for the day, they'll release any excess back into the watercourse. Evidently, they're not greedy with their water needs. Which reminds me of the Native American saying, "A frog does not drink up the pond in which it lives." The hundred-plus golf course operators in the Valley of the Sun, take note.

Mission accomplished, walking back down-wash to the river, I stumbled upon a rusted steel animal trap, anchored by its chain in the dirt, immovable. May this sacred area never know any more of that barbarity, I murmured. From beastliness I went to beauty: a grove of catalpas, desert willows, blooms pendulous and palest purple with a subtle fragrance that needed up-nearness to know it.

Having got back to camp quite early in the day, I summoned up courage to shampoo the matted mop that passed for my head of hair. Pre-shampooing, it was a hairy proposition even for a horse-comb. However, the neat thing about this anything but neat state of affairs (or a-hairs) was that I had had the freedom of not having to do anything about it until I was good and ready. That is, being on a seven-day solo in the back of beyond, if I wanted to be a wild man (or better, a wild child), I could be one. Because all of our adult lives are spent under the tyranny of neighbours, under that appalling yoke of What will people think?, this knotted unkempt hair was to me the symbol of unfettered freedom.

Anyhow, I took the gallon milk jug scoop to the spring and, hoping the nesting doves overhead wouldn't be unnerved by my splashing, I showered and shampooed—and shivered. For all the symbolism of a wild and woolly hair-do, I must admit to having felt fresh as a daisy — and rather invigorated — after the hygiene treatment. Pity there was nobody around to appreciate it.

Yet more journal writing morning and afternoon. Quite the taskmaster, this journal. But always well-worth it, in retrospect. Useful as a Sonoran chronicle and providing more desert material for my readings, this one makes the eighth solo trek account; there were two dry years when I wrote nothing.

I've discovered that by hugging the cliff on the other side of the path to the spring, I can spare at least one egg-hatching whitewing dove some disruption of her maternal duties. Unhappily, tho', on one water-trip I barged in on a coachwhip snake's making a meal of a bluish-green tree lizard. The snake saw me, let go of the lizard, and flew from the rough bark of the willow, site of the dinner date, onto the muddy path near where I was walking. I jumped back instinctively. The lizard, quite a fat fellow, scuttled off up into the tree — and lived to leap again another day. I was sorry that I'd spoiled the snake's supper — and no doubt it was sorrier. What a pain in the ass we are to the wild kingdom, however well-meaning we may be.

Back on the bank, I gathered up a fistful of fallen mesquite beanpods (*péchitas* in Sonora, Mexico) and set about pounding them with a proper *mano* that had surfaced from the fine sand on the floor of the cave. It gave me pause to think that here I was at the close of the twentieth century holding and using a *mano* that other hands perhaps 500 years ago had held and used — most likely on mesquite beans, too. My pounding, then, was not without a touch of reverence and, beating back that acquisitive urge again (but not without difficulty), I made up my mind that the *mano* would be returned to the cave where, well-hidden, it stood a fair chance of spending another 500 years there — if not eternity. I boiled up the smashed and sticky pods over a campfire. The result, when strained, was a sweet-sour beverage long known to the Mexican people as *atole*. An interesting drink that could easily grow on one — if there were no coffee or tea or Koolaid lemonade powder around. The same could be said for roasted jojoba nuts, as a coffee bean substitute. Or Mormon tea from the wild plant *Ephedra*.

Early evening a storm, announced by the mumblings and

grumblings of thunder and the flashings and flickerings of lightning — and with all the makings of a drenching downpour, trundled in. I battened down the hatches, ate hastily, and repaired to the cave where I was viewer to a powerful picture show of the incoming storm. A half-rainbow straddled the grey and lowering clouds. But it was one of those southwestern summer anomalies — a dry squall with a few meagre droplets of rain. All show, no staying power.

Before dark I walked upwash to the grand-daddy of a giant cactus which for me had always served as a guide to the last leg of the hike to the river cove. Many-armed, tall as a two-storey house, this one had probably been around since the first Independence Day — without exaggeration. I thought I'd pay my respects to it. What I didn't expect was the whole family of gila woodpeckers with four or five young but fledged members a-squawking and a-flapping around the prickly green columns. I stayed dead still at the base of the saguaro, gazing up at their antics. They ignored me. The raven and the carpenter bird (as the Mexicans call the woodpecker) share the prize as the most raucous-voiced of the desert avians.

Before calling it a day, I again saw the elfish owl — or was it an owlish elf? — in the mesquite tree. And tonight there was another one, its mate perhaps, calling close by.

Slept only fitfully — and, dammit, was annoyed by the basso profundo of those idiot bullfrogs. The sound drifted maddeningly all the way to where I had moved to be rid of it. Tossing and turning, I made a vow that this was the last night I'd put up with it.

Friday July 20th 1990

Sticking by the vow, I dismantled the tent after getting up. There was no sense of loss in shifting camp. I'd been there one week already. The sky was clouded over, Old Sol having a bit of trouble forcing his way thro' it. This would make hiking out easier, though. With three days still left, I made a decision to head for an assured freshwater source and lie low, reading, writing, rambling, ruminating. Depending on rides along remote roads, I was hoping to be back home by Sunday evening. "Hope springs eternal in the human breast."

The gnats and no-see-ums were markedly numerous and aggressive this morning — another valid reason for leaving. A belted kingfisher flashed by, skimming the river as I was packing up. A mourning dove, doing what she was meant to do, cooed mournfully in the willow above me. Was she sorry to see me go? I doubt it. Nevertheless, the nearest nesting whitewing had grown used to my passing underneath her and simply stayed put on her sparse nest of twigs. It's not nice to be a source of terror to wild things all the time, so I was happy about that. Tanked up with springwater for the journey — and gave thanks to the source — for I couldn't have remained there a week without it. Noticed freshly emerged mushrooms — or toadstools — in the earthy bank above the small pool I'd scooped out of the sand. Quite a few were popping up in the desert, too. I'd seen inkcaps and even puffballs. In an arid land, that had to be a measure for the amount of rain that'd fallen lately. Marvellous to think how those fungi spores tough it out and stay vital for hot and dry months on end.

Made my farewells, with gratitude, to the peaceful place that had been home for seven days, shouldered the backpack (which still seemed heavy), and got a grip on the sack of crushed aluminum. That wasn't light either, but I had to lug it out of that pristine land. Breakfast on the hoof included hackberries at the upper end of the wash. Madrecita had done me proud with her dietary supplements this trip — no preservatives, either. Two jackrabbits and a lot of lizards gave me a sendoff. At about eight o'clock, off I marched. An hour later I stashed the pack in shade and explored a bleached chalk gully that led me by and by to the river. Ran into two deer, both solitary, on the way there — both of them big does, one drinking, the other taking shade. They bounded off at great speed and their clear tracks in the damp sand enabled me to foot-measure the length of each bound, three and four yards, no less. On reaching the river, I clambered up a sandstone cliff for an overview — and at the top stepped right into the midst of a rambling Indian ruin terraced up and away from the brink of the escarpment; several had excavated wall sections. This must have been a sizeable community, perhaps a whole town.

By 11:30 I was back in the safety zone of sweetwater and in a short while came to a pool. Enough hiking for the day. High noon was nigh and it was hotter than the dickens. I didn't care to budge another inch. Set up camp in a mesquite bosque above the creek's flood level. Good to unload and relax — but better yet to sink like a stone into the waterhole.

To go with lunch I brewed up a pan of tea over white ash mesquite coals, savouring the acrid smell of woodsmoke so warmly associated with camping. Funny how it always follows you, though — making the eyes smart, the nose run, and the throat cough. With back to a lichen-painted rock, I spent a few hours writing up the journal — and then, growing weary of words, went for a walk upstream. Learned that I was still a half-hour away from the mouth of the side canyon that I was eager to explore and so thought to move camp nearer to this spot. This I did after dinner, situating myself in a stand of arrowweed, hidden from the jeep road which might be used, being the weekend. Though still in the outback, I was surely in off-road vehicle and cow country again. The creek flowed more spottily here — but I made sure there was enough to drink and for primitive ablutions.

People have now and then asked me about the problem of giardia, an intestinal bug occasionally found in natural streams. Many would never dream of drinking straight from them. Their choice, of course. All I know is that countless are the creeks and rivers that I've drunk from without ill effects. It'll be a sad day when I won't belly down to a desert creek and drink my fill.

Because the sky was moderately clear by dark, I didn't put up the tent, simply laid out the broad plastic sheet and rolled out pad and sleeping bag on it. No ants in the neighborhood, either. A quiet night beneath the twinkling stars was being looked forward to. But it started out badly, first with the bellowing of cattle closeby and then, infuriatingly, with the sound of gunshots. Some imbeciles at the camping area maybe a mile farther up were shooting into the darkness. Welcome back to what they call Civilization, G.P.

But this was mild stuff compared to what awaited me.

More shots, silence, the noise of a car engine coming closer —and then the sweep of headlights thro' the willow trees across from me where the jeep road lay. Loud voices, young males, one of them shouting, "Stop! Quick! Get it!" Javelina grunts from below in the streambed and then, oh, God, two rifle shots in rapid succession. "Back up! Back up!" I heard one yell. And now, sick at them shooting at wildlife and fearful of being hit by a stray bullet, I flattened face down on the ground, head wrapped in both arms. It was nightmarish and all the more so having just come from the sanity and peace of the river.

Two courses of action lay open to me: either to shout out and confront them with their madness or to stay down, unseen and silent. Suspecting that they were drunk and thus irrational, I chose to do nothing except to pray that they would soon be gone. My heart thudded like mad as I lay there pressed close into the soft earth. The javelina had fled into the night. I don't think any were hit. More shouts and curses, the starting up of the engine, the wild waving of a flashlight with one of these louts going ahead of the truck on foot to guide it down the rough track.

And finally they were gone, thank God. Though worn out by the exertions of the day, it took me forever to get to sleep. How incredible it was, I thought, that this brutishness should have happened so near to me — and when my mind and spirit were least prepared for it. In D. H. Lawrence's poem, "Mountain Lion," he wrote of a sudden encounter with two armed men in the mountains of New Mexico, one of them carrying a puma he had shot. A line from this poem leapt vividly to mind:

> Men! Two men! Men, the only animal in the world to fear....

That I always knew — but now I had experienced it.

Saturday July 21st 1990

The cry of a poorwill came first into my waking consciousness, then a merry medley of other birdsong. I thought of last night's peril and was glad for the peace of the moment — and for a new day. Didn't bother with a fire for coffee this a.m. Made do with a lemonade drink and a grapefruit. After breakfast I headed up the side canyon, aware that this would be the last morning meander of my solo. I had a vague recollection of there being a swim hole in the area and wanted to see if I could find it again. Two hours of determined boulder hopping didn't bring me to any idyllic pool, but there was a steady flow of water and where it came up against the cliff-face, a place to dip and wallow in. More snakes seen this a.m. than all trip long — an adult garter snake and a wriggling baby one, a coachwhip and two grey racers, one of whose supple body made that odd whine as it streaked away. Too many cows in this canyon — they'd stunted a lot of cottonwood and willow saplings with their munching. Riparian habitat needs to regenerate its deciduous trees. Cattle defeat that re-growth.

Some handsome Apache plume flowers aong the way — and a verdant dump of six- to seven-foot horse's tail mullein which loves a floodplain niche. I should try those pioneer pan scourers on my pair of carbon-encrusted cooking pans. Battered and stained but tried and true, those two have served me long and loyally.

When I got back to camp after roaming for a good four hours, I had a light lunch. (Quite a change for chowhound Platts — but my appetite had dwindled in the last few days; less food plus daily hiking has meant a trimming down. Seems these solos get the fat off the bod as well as the soul. Watch out, developers. He's mean and lean now.) Since I calculated being within forty-five minutes' walk of the road out, I thought it'd be a sound idea to make a dry run — without the pack — but carry out the sackful of aluminum cans which had amassed into a dead weight. And then cache them until I came back with a vehicle someday. That would save me a bit of sweat on the morrow. This I did, picking up more cans en route. When I do this — and I do it often — I regard it as a small gift back to Nature for the much greater gift of beauty she has given to me. It's as simple as that. A string of beer cans that I gathered up had been recently tossed by some yahoo — and yet only a handful of cars had been on the jeep track in the past week. How can one win?

Even as I was burying the bag of cans in brushwood, the sky to the northeast had become black and glowering. The storm would be upon me at any minute. I was relieved that I'd put up the tent in a sheltered grove before leaving. Half-way back down the creek, the wind and the rain hit both me and the trees full force. I broke into a trot, not wanting a flashflood crashing down on my tail. Though sagging badly, the tent was still standing — with the bedding dry inside. Covering myself and the gear still outside with the clear plastic sheet (a salvation), I huddled beneath it, splattered by large drops of rain. The storm front blew by quickly but another came on its heels — more rain, this time harder driven. By now I was snug inside the tent and, with darkness falling, set for the night. I was tired out and fell asleep straightaway.

Some animal shrieked in the middle of the night, and I woke up but only briefly.

Sunday July 22nd 1990

The final day. Thoughts turned to the other world, that of man. Coyotes sang their farewell from the direction of the river. I answered them in like fashion. Packed up damp. But since I planned to spend most of the day finishing off the journal and writing letters under the sycamores at the roadhead, there'd be ample time for sun-drying the equipment. Curiously, despite two cloudbursts, the creek did not flood — perhaps because the earth was already soft and yielding. There is no accounting for Madrecita's caprices.

A lone coyote padded across the creek bed fifty yards up from me. It paid me no heed and melted into the undergrowth. "Backpack Ho! Time to go!" I was where I wanted to be in half an hour. No people there, just bawling cattle and a single vulture swaying high on a dead branch above the stinking carcase of a Hereford cow. I laid out the plastic sheet, tent, and towel to dry in the sun — and collected up more trash. Campers had degraded this car-reachable area, sad to say: ugly fire-rings, chopped trees (even a live cottonwood), inevitable garbage. Yet beauty won out in spite of *Homo rapiens*. Here and there a pure white, yellow-eyed prickly poppy (the cowboy's fried egg), a royal blue trailing windmill, and a summer-flowering devil's claw with its orchid-like bloom egg-yolk in colour.

Man passes away, Nature persists.

And so my state of aloneness, on this tenth solo trek, came

to a close. In only a few hours I would be back in contact with my fellow man again — after being away from him for nine days. The social side of me looked forward to that — although there'd been no missing that contact in my solitude.

If anything disturbs me about modern society, it is its fear of being alone. As though aloneness were loneliness! I suppose the fear stems from a deep reluctance to look inward — and the symptoms of that fear are extroversion and distraction — anything rather than the facing up to oneself. Thus solitude is a thing to be avoided like the plague because, when alone and without the myriad distractions offered by society, what else can one do but face up to oneself? And that appears to be a frightening prospect to most. I saw an ad not long ago (I think it was for some high-tech cellular phone). The headline read, YOU NEED NEVER BE ALONE AGAIN. What does that say? It says to me that the adman's idea of heaven is my idea of hell.

There's no better way for me to end this journal than with this poem by D. H. Lawrence.

> I never know what people mean when they complain of loneliness.
> To be alone is one of life's greatest delights,
> Thinking one's own thoughts, doing one's own little jobs,
> Seeing the world beyond
> And feeling oneself uninterrupted
> in the rooted connection
> With the centre of all things.

Geoffrey Platts
Arizona
July 22nd 1990

The author stands up for what he believes. He leads a community picket annually at an 8,000+-acre golf development near Carefree, Arizona. Here he stands a solitary vigil against a 1,200-acre development in Scottsdale (January 1981).
(Photo by Bob Johnstone, courtesy *Scottsdale Progress*)

Afterword

Sentiment without action is the ruin of the soul.

— Edward Abbey

It is one thing to sing the praises of the natural world. It is quite another to rally to the defense of it. But now we have arrived at an ecological point so very critical that all who get pleasure from Nature's gifts — of beauty, silence, and solitude — must, in some form or other, take immediate steps to defend her:

"Pay your rent — work for the Earth."

There is now no time to lose, no more shying from that personal and collective covenant to be made with Nature. This is because the natural systems of land, air, and water are everywhere at grave risk. Nor can they be made whole again without our resolute and concerted action on their behalf. And so these times call on us, each and every one, to tithe for the Earth in the way we are best able.

The realms of environmental involvement to choose from are varied, ranging from volunteer stewardship, giving or raising funds to preserve habitat, recycling at the home or community level, eco-educating of youth within the family or in the school, supporting of conservation groups both local and national, writing activism (such as letters to editors, members of congress, state legislators, hometown council members), signature-gathering for petitions or initiatives, testifying at public hearings — to peaceful protest.

In short, it is vital for all of us to do *something*. To put our shoulders to the wheel of life. Without further delay.

Above all, this labour of love for the natural world calls for us to start simplifying our lives — to pare away the excess, to cut out the waste, to come to see the value in less and the fatal fallacy in more. *Multum in parvo*. Much in little.

Both individually and societally, this will require a paradigm shift — a dramatic turning around in our cultural thinking. Yet, in the end, the Earth will be the healthier for our new leanness of living and simplicity of spirit. And so shall we.

"Come, my friends, 'tis not too late to seek a newer world."

—Tennyson

Colophon

The text is set in 11/13 Palatino using Xerox's Ventura Publisher running on an 80286 computer by Sho-Tronics, Phoenix. Book design by Jack Grenard. Negatives by Parkwest Graphics, Scottsdale, Arizona. Printing and binding by McNaughton & Gunn, Saline, Michigan, on fifty-pound recycled, acid-free JB Offset stock. The publisher gratefully acknowledges the generous use of the Foothills Community Foundation's laser printer for preliminary production in Carefree.

Additional copies, $10.50 postpaid. (Price good through 1992.) Available from Carefree Communications, Inc., Box 5268,